Training in Organisations

Training
in Organisations

A Cost-Benefit Analysis

JOHN TALBOT

GOWER

Published by
Gower Publishing Limited
Wey Court East
Union Road
Farnham
Surrey, GU9 7PT
England

Gower Publishing Company
Suite 420
101 Cherry Street
Burlington,
VT 05401-4405
USA

www.gowerpublishing.com

British Library Cataloguing in Publication Data
Talbot, J. R. (John R.)
  Training in organisations : a cost-benefit analysis.
  1. Employees--Training of--Cost effectiveness.
  I. Title
  658.3'12404-dc22

Library of Congress Cataloging-in-Publication Data
Talbot, J. R. (John R.)
  Training in organisations : a cost-benefit analysis / John Talbot.
      p. cm.
  Includes bibliographical references and index.
  ISBN 978-0-566-09210-7 (hbk) -- ISBN 978-1-4094-2361-4
(ebook) 1. Employees--Training of--Cost effectiveness. I. Title.
  HF5549.5.T7T253 2011
  658.3'124--dc22

                                                    2010048035

ISBN   978-0-566-09210-7 (hbk)
ISBN   978-1-4094-2361-4 (ebk)

Printed and bound in Great Britain by the
MPG Books Group, UK

Contents

List of Figures

Preface – A Word About the Trainer

In the twenty-first century the word 'trainer' may well evoke the concept of a personal coach to help with athletic type exercises, and in the plural, the footgear worn to indulge in them. It is not a title used so often these days when 'HR' specialists and various consultants appear on the organisation charts, and yet it covers a multitude of activities and implies the need for quite sophisticated skills. At first glance, there is a feeling that 'presentation skills' are sufficient, and many a novice is sent on a course so entitled, in order to become more professional. Unfortunately, the content is often based on designing more and better electronic visuals, which require a darkened room and a well-behaved audience!

So what are the real skills a trainer needs? First of all, they begin long before any contact is made with the learner:

Diagnosis

What is the person or persons not doing that you want them to do? Or what do you want them to stop doing?

Were they once able to do it in a satisfactory manner? If so, what has changed in the environment? Or do they need more practice? Training may not be the answer.

Setting Behavioural Objectives

The skill is in not being seduced into using words like 'understand,' 'appreciate,' 'have better knowledge of,' or accepting some manager's insistence that they need to change their attitude to something or other. None of these can be measured; objectives must be observable and measurable in order that the learning experience may be evaluated.

Planning and Design

Decisions need to be made when a physical skill is to learned, that is, how to involve realistic practice while ensuring learners are not allowed to handle potentially dangerous situations before they are ready. The ever-present 'health and safety' issues apply.

An appropriate division of time between demonstration and practice, and a sense of how much to 'feed' the learner before indigestion occurs, is learned from experience and obtaining feedback often enough during the process.

Design of a 'course' for a group of people is similar, and just a bit more complicated. How do we involve everyone in a participative experience without losing 'slower' learners and boring others? Simple…help them to learn with and from each other by designing small group activities to discuss specific topics and report back to the plenary group.

There are pitfalls however:

- DON'T give each group the same topic or questions, it then becomes a competition.

- DON'T have the 'right' answers already prepared, what an insult!

- DO plan to check up on each group after about two minutes to ensure they have understood the task, and then give a time check five minutes before the deadline.

- DO try and have all groups in one large room for easier monitoring, and to raise the energy level.

Relationship Building

Do not underestimate the value of 'getting to know you'. Time spent doing this will save time later and establish an atmosphere of mutual respect in an adult fashion. Engaging with the learner, one to one and in groups, is a skill to be developed, perhaps by modelling those you have watched do it well in the past. A technique in groups (again divided into smaller units) is to pose such questions as 'Who are we?' 'Why are we here?' which may even get a laugh – which suggests yet another critical skill…

Demonstrating a Sense of Humour

To demonstrate a sense of humour you do not have to be a stand-up comic, but express warmth and a sense that we can't be serious all the time and maybe the task at hand is not (unless it is, of course) a matter of life and death!

Presentation Skills

Powerpoint is all very well, but it doesn't help you to engage and encourages leaving 'any questions?' to the end. It may either be forgotten by then or, unanswered when it occurred, be a distraction for the intervening time. Often, flipchart notes can outline your plan and be informal enough to be amended by the trainer or the learner. Another advantage of flipchart notes is that they require no electrical support and, if your training location has no easels, there is a giant 'Post-It' version which can be safely stuck on any surface without removing plaster or paint.

Finally, you are your own visual aid: appropriate dress is usually more formal than that of your participants. It tells them you're taking them seriously and have taken time with your appearance. Also, moving about the room makes you more accessible and real.

How Do we Acquire these Skills?

Maybe there is an appropriate course available. Check whether its objectives are observable and measurable. Or, maybe an 'apprenticeship' can be arranged, watching and learning from others who are recognised professional practitioners. Good luck!

J. Anne McQuade

Acknowledgements

I would like to thank the many people who have continued to stimulate my thinking in the training field, particularly the many friends and colleagues from emas Consultants since its establishment in 1971. Special thanks are due to Anne McQuade for ongoing help with the manuscript and contribution of the Prologue and the Last Word.

Final work on the manuscript was completed thanks to the professional work of Janet Farmer whose secretarial work formed a vital part of the development of the emas group of companies.

Chapters 9–15 are based on the original work of C.D. Ellis with whom the original publication *Analysis and Costing of Company Training* was developed.

1

Scope of Training

For many years, training has been seen as an extension to the educational process within business and administration. This has been reflected even in the titles of managers working in the field with the result that attitudes within business have been strongly conditioned to accept a traditional teaching approach. Companies appointed 'education officers' who were inevitably concerned mainly with the use of relevant courses at technical colleges. Training is thought about in terms of courses. Even outside assessors asked for training records rather than evidence of learning and improvement. The learning process was seen as something which almost unavoidably took place outside the business. Emphasis in discussion was on means of arranging release for study and, even in areas which were totally outside the scope of further education, first thoughts were to arrange suitable training 'off-the-job'.

This educational bias is still found, both within industries and the civil service. Publications dealing with the training of various categories of workers are frequently little more than an examination of the educational background required. There are still suggestions that the effectiveness of training in key areas, such as that of engineering apprentices or commercial trainees, depends on the facilities provided for day release on expensive courses.

This growth of educational awareness within industry is, of course, entirely desirable, but it must be recognised as only a first step towards the establishment of effective training throughout industry, commerce and administration. Unless a broader view of training is adopted, there is some danger in any new training development getting off to a false start and being thought of as only very marginal value by line managers. It is important that training energy is not dissipated or training efforts misconstrued at this vital period of the country's economic challenges. Stimulated by the activities of government initiatives and human resource managers, most managers now recognise that training is vital, but if too much effort is channelled into apparently academic and unproductive areas, this enthusiasm could easily evaporate, with tragic results in terms of productivity and adaptation to change.

The key requirements for trainers in the immediate future will be the ability to use their educational skills to influence fundamentally the development of learning within industry in both the long and short term. Effective learning is now more than ever an essential element in the management of human resources and in the use and adaptation of material development. Learning problems within industry must be clearly analysed and their implications for training made clear. In many ways this requires new educational skills, very different from the classroom techniques of the past. In spite of generally derogatory references to 'sitting next to Nellie', much crucial learning must take place in the job situation and techniques must be found to control and manage it. Except in certain cases of lack of knowledge, opting for off-the-job training will not necessarily provide adequate solutions.

The necessary change of emphasis is a reflection of the fact that training, as it is now understood, is expected to contribute to a much wider range of organisational problems than previously. It is, therefore, important to draw a clear distinction between the more traditional problems and the problems of the future. This will illustrate the greater integration required of any training operation as well as the wide range of skills needed by the trainer.

Traditional Problems

Training has normally been expected to contribute to four main types of problem; lack of knowledge, preparation for promotion, adjustment to new organisational structures, and unsatisfactory performance.

LACK OF KNOWLEDGE

This is the classic situation and will always be of very great importance. It is the area where traditional teaching methods may still be highly effective and where training away from the job can be most easily organised. The process of direct transfer of knowledge will be steadily improved as new techniques are developed. Programmed learning will make an increasing contribution alongside other tutorial, IT and classroom techniques.

Despite its continuing importance, however, it must not be allowed to influence unduly the total approach to training which must consider other problems at the same time.

PREPARATION FOR PROMOTION

Training in this area is again of longstanding importance although sometimes referred to by other names, such as management development. Part of the problem here may well be lack of knowledge, but it has been clearly recognised in this area for sometime that job experience and career patterning is essential. However, no ideal formula has been found for approaching the situation and some of the traditional concepts, such as systems of job rotation, may need to be changed.

ADJUSTMENT TO NEW ORGANISATIONAL STRUCTURES

The explanation of organisation change is a growing part of any training manager's job. It is important, but basically a fairly straightforward exercise in communication. Limitations in this area have very often been related to the lack of any early integration of training thinking with the reorganisation process itself. This has led to effective efforts being somewhat frustrated by their greater concern with explaining the results of change than with influencing the process of change. Structural changes in organisation have frequently been considered separately from changes required in individuals. The aim must be to bring these projects together. For instance, if decision levels are changed, those concerned have to be equipped to make decisions at new levels.

LOW INDIVIDUAL PERFORMANCE

This is frequently related to lack of knowledge, but by no means always so. Training must always make an effective contribution to improving skills, knowledge and attitudes related to individual competence. In many cases this is a question of retraining often of mature adults, with all the problems that this involves. Much useful development has taken place in this area recently, but here also, perhaps rather too much attention has been paid to traditional teaching approaches rather than to the total adjustment of individuals to situations which have developed beyond their competence.

Training contributions in these areas will always be important, but many companies have devised reasonably effective means of meeting requirements of this type and training managers should find it relatively easy to obtain information which will help to provide solutions in their own situations. The important thing is that these traditional areas may not be the priority areas for new developments or the priority areas in terms of cost and pay-off. For instance, lack of individual competence may still be widespread and important, but not necessarily the cause of major organisational difficulty. It is more disturbing that the necessary degree of competence often appears to be present but is poorly used. Similarly, training designed to attack the problems behind structural change may be more important than training concerned purely with adjustment to a new organisation.

The training manager of the future will need to make a much more thorough analysis of the fundamental organisational problems facing the business if there is to be real success in making contributions to productivity and profitability. The provision of new routine training answers to traditional problems will not be sufficient. The requirement is for a much more extensive diagnostic skill which looks behind the learning processes of individuals and of groups and assesses the impact of this on the business's need for growth and adjustment.

New Problems

Although many of the techniques will be the same, training should now be expected to contribute to much broader problems concerned with both organisational effectiveness and individual effectiveness.

INTEGRATION OF MANAGEMENT EFFORT

Many managerial practices and organisational structures have not been particularly conducive to the effective use of human resources and the best integration of effort. Learning in this area has been relatively slow. It requires fundamental changes in attitudes and approach and is a very worthy target for training activity. Integrated development can be stimulated by the use of recognised standards such as ISO 2001:2008 and Investors in People. Individuals and the organisation are developed at the same time. Team development is encouraged as well as individual learning. Challenges are met successfully, developing a culture that can respond to future challenges.[1]

CLARIFICATION OF INDIVIDUAL GOALS AND THEIR LINK WITH MANAGEMENT OBJECTIVES

This is again an organisational problem, but one which is really concerned with consolidating learning and directing development of the whole group.

DEVELOPMENT OF NEW THINKING

Training which emphasises the teaching of accepted knowledge tends to overlook the equally important need to check the spread of ideas and practices that are likely to stifle new thinking and attitudes. Training should challenge accepted thinking and attack the conditioning of the past which acts as a major brake on growth and the use of resources. The training techniques are those referred to in the jargon as 'unfreezing' processes. This term does, in fact, give a vivid impression of what is required to swing an organisation in a new direction.

Redirection of training effort of this kind is primarily related to a search for techniques which influence fundamental problems of management and organisation. It requires not only a change in direction but also a change in scale. The more general objectives require a more wholesale approach. Everyone becomes involved. The emphasis is on training the business rather than training individuals within it.

Thinking of this kind completely alters the starting point for training managers. They are no longer teachers in industry. They are managers contributing a special skill to the diagnosis of basic business and organisational problems. They use educational techniques, but the real skill is in translating them into business practices. The scope of training becomes much broader and its management much more akin to that of other areas of industrial development.

---

1 Arnold Toynbee. *A Study of History:*

Growth (that is, development) occurs when the response to a particular challenge is not only successful in itself but provokes a further challenge which is not only successful in itself but provokes a further challenge which again meets with a successful response.

This approach is an Action Learning approach.

Role of the Trainer

It is often argued that training must start at the top and it may well be that many training problems can be traced to bad management. It is often possible for the outside training consultant to start at the top and may usually have sufficient status for recommendations to be accepted. The internal trainer, however, cannot and should not emulate the outside consultants who can determine their own point of entry into the organisation. The trainer has a position in the organisation already established – usually somewhere in the middle. The approach must be from this position. The skill must be to build a basis for action. A trainer must have a learning and integration process as shown in Figure 1.1. Initially, the identification and interpretation of problems may be at or below the trainer's level. This will demonstrate skill in the area in such a way and on such problems that the operation will naturally and rapidly expand from the base focal point to the broader policy and organisation problems which are in the top management area. Further crucial developments in training may stem from the top but the approach will in fact be a 'realistic' one tackling problems at all levels. From this point onwards the trainer should have little worry about the level of training or the credibility of his position in the hierarchy. The problems will dictate the levels of operation.

Figure 1.1   Developing the trainer

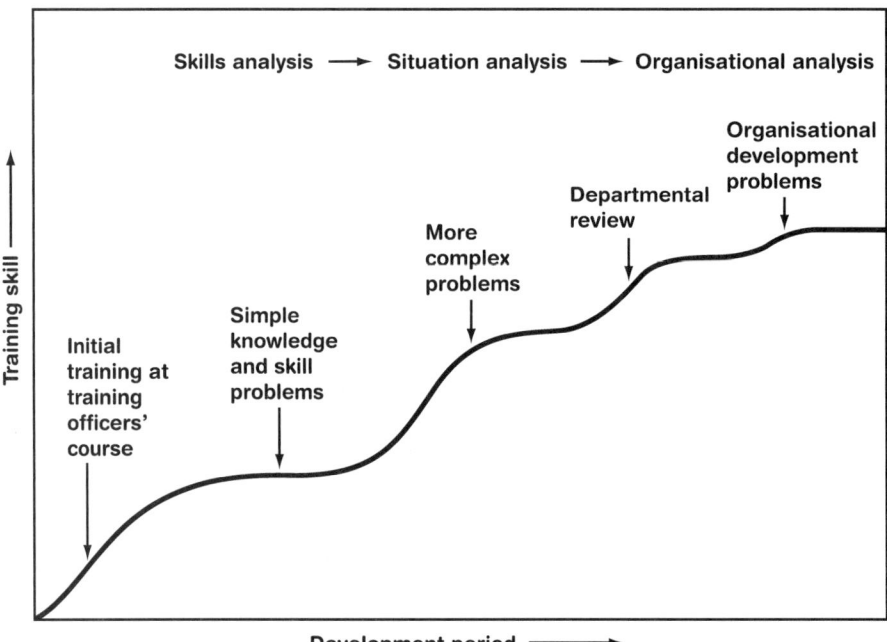

Because of this it is very clear that the trainer's first approach to the identification of problems is crucial. Breadth and depth of thinking at this early stage may well determine their own future and the level and nature of the function's contribution for some time to come.

This will enable the company to benefit from a total approach to training not by looking immediately for 'top-level' problems and top-level connection, but by tackling clearly definable training problems well and following them through – to the top.

The responsibilities of the trainer are most succinctly described by means of a job description. Two such job descriptions are given in Appendix 1 to this chapter and define the duties of trainers at two levels. The position of training supervisor (engineering) provides for the translation of the work of the technical development training manager into the company situation.

Appendix 1a: Job Description – Training Manager

TECHNICAL DEVELOPMENT DEPARTMENT

The technical development training manager is responsible for the development and maintenance of a training organisation which will meet the internal requirements of the department and anticipate and ensure provision for the technical training requirements arising from development projects. The job will provide the foundation and focus for technical training developments throughout the company. Particular duties are detailed below.

TRAINING FOR DEVELOPMENT PROJECTS

- Appraisal of the training implications of development projects.

- Systematic integration of training arrangements within the projects facilitating effective translation from the development to operational stage.

This will involve:

- Identification and analysis of skills, knowledge and attitudes required at all levels.

- Formulation of training programmes based on this analysis.

- Liaison with managers in carrying out the necessary local training.

- Liaison with manufacturers in obtaining information on specialised training.

- Preparation of training manuals and other training aids.

- Organisation of training courses for staff.

- Constant evaluation of training arrangements in terms of cost and learning effectiveness.

- Avoidance of unnecessary learning problems by influencing projects at the design stage.

TRAINING FOR TECHNICAL CHANGE

- Appraisal of the training implications of major changes within the technical area, such as instrumentation and control development or changes in work measurement techniques, and the preparation of appropriate training measures to facilitate them.

- Liaison with other training managers to ensure that the latest developments throughout the training field are fully utilised in the technical field.

TRAINING FOR DEVELOPMENT PROJECTS

Carry out a continuous review and analysis of management training needs and organise or recommend appropriate action. This will involve:

- Identification of major management problems and their interpretation in training terms.

- Identification of individual training needs.

- Identification of group training needs.

- Organisation of meetings, conferences and courses designed to improve management performance and facilitate organisational development.

- Assisting in the development of effective management objective setting and other techniques contributing to systematic training within the job.

- Preparation of management development lists for the department.

- Organisation of systematic introductory training for all jobs.

- Liaison with appropriate consultants in the management training field in obtaining advice and, where necessary, help in running training sessions.

OTHER DEPARTMENTAL TRAINING

- Ensure that training needs are effectively analysed and appropriate training programmes put into effect.

EDUCATION

- Administration of the company's education scheme in the department.

- Advising managers on the suitability of courses available.

- Promotion of the company's interest in the field of further education.

TRAINING BUDGET

- Prepare the training budget and ensure costs are kept within it.

Appendix 1b: Job Description – Training Supervisor (Engineering)

The Training Supervisor (Engineering) is directly responsible for the development of training programmes for supervisors, craftsmen, and apprentices, in line with long-term company plans and local requirements. They are concerned with maintaining close liaison with local colleges to ensure the relevance of courses to company needs. Specific duties are detailed below.

APPRENTICES

- Selection and recruitment of apprentices in accordance with forward plans.

- Planning and administration of integrated training programmes.

- Systematic appraisal at each stage of training.

CRAFTSMEN

- Initially, to analyse systematically on an individual and a group basis, the training and retraining requirements of fitters and electricians to meet anticipated company and local technical developments.

- To arrange appropriate training both 'in-house' and by selected external courses, for example, instrumentation and control training.

SUPERVISION

In consultation with the training manager, systematically to analyse individual training needs. To arrange appropriate training by:

- Secondments.

- Guided projects.

- Formal courses on specific techniques.

- Objective setting exercises designed to involve engineering supervision together with other departmental supervision thus broadening experience.

MACHINE UTILISATION

- To maintain close liaison with the development training manager on forward plans for the introduction of new machines.

- To be concerned with the training manager and the development training officer in the planning and implementation of training programmes associated with new and modified machinery including the compilation of machine manuals and fault diagnosis schedules.

TRAINING TECHNIQUES

- Keep abreast of latest developments in techniques for craft training and recommend suitable applications, for example, programmed and on-line learning for apprentices.

FURTHER EDUCATION

- Closely supervise the progress of apprentices and others studying at local colleges and maintain a continuous contact with those apprentices undergoing full-time first year training so as to ensure the integration of academic training with work experience.

2

Defining Investment in People

A simple and straightforward way of defining where there is a need for training is the production of Skills Matrices. They are a sound but simple means of highlighting the skills gaps in an organisation and identifying the needs of training or planned experience in key areas.

An example of a skills matrix is shown in Figure 2.1; Competence matrix.

Potential Dangers

The 'skills mapping' technique is extremely helpful and constructive provided the map can be kept simple. Complication and over-elaboration can distort and destroy the whole purpose of the exercise.

The major danger is confusing the definition of performance and learning needs with appraisal. The need is to recognise skills gaps in order to fill them, to meet important training needs. There should be no personal rating of performance other than the need for further learning or training. Appraisal is a different process requiring confidentiality. It is a completely personal process, described separately later in this book.

The consequences of public appraisal, often linked to remuneration, can lead to a wide range of disasters. The complete implosion of some organisations, such as Enron, is sometimes attributed to so-called personal and management development schemes, publicly linking pay to personal appraisal. The consequences can be:

- blatant corruption and cheating;

- unnecessary and destructive competition;

- thorough undermining of team work in a battle for individual 'gold stars'.

Management Standards

Major Management Standards provide an excellent and widely accepted framework for recognising and meeting training and learning needs. The principles of ISO 9000 speak for themselves in many ways and are reviewed in some detail in Chapter 8. Whilst focusing on managerial skills, they provide a framework for high-quality skill development at all levels.

The Investors in People Standard speaks for itself and the basic requirements are set out in Appendix 2b. A comparison between the two is summarised in Figure 2.2 'Standards compared'.

The use and purpose of ISO 9000 is summarised in Appendix 2a 'Managing through ISO 9001:2008'.

Figure 2.1   Competence matrix

Name	Title	Storekeeping	Packing	I.T Literacy	Purchasing	Selling	Cust Relations	Telephone	Negotiation	Bookkeeping	Management	Supervision	Dr Licence	F/L Trucks	H&S Training	H&S Awareness	Dangerous Goods	Manual Handling	Deliveries	Marketing	Stock Checking	First Aid	Auditor	ISO Awareness	Comments
Charles	Commercial Manager	X	X	X	X	X	X	X	X		X	X	X		X		X	X	X	X	X		X	X	
Raymond	Accounts Manager		X	X		X	X	X	X	X	X	X	X		X				X		X			X	
John	Stores Assistant	X	X	X			X	X					X	X	X	X	X	X	X	X				X	
Carol	Accounts Assistant		X	X		X				X			X	X	X	X								X	
David	Sales Manager	X	X	X	X	X	X	X	X			X	X	X	X		X	X	X	X	X			X	
Steve	Stores Manager	X	X	X		X	X	X	X		X	X	X	X	X	X	X	X		X	X	X	X	X	
Ian	Stores Assistant	X	X	X		X	X	X			X	X	X	0	X	X	X	X		X	X	X		X	forklift training TBA
Sonia	Sales Executive			X	X	X	X	X	X				X		X				X					X	
Jason	Sales Executive	X	X	X	X	X	X	X	X						X			X	X	X				X	
Gordon	Stores Assistant	X	X	X	X	X	X	X					X	0	X		X	X	X	X	X			X	forklift training TBA
Edward	Sales Executive	X	X	X	X	X	X	X					X		X		X	X	X	X	X			X	
Patrick	CEO		X			X	X	X		X	X	X	X		X					X			X	X	
Dawn	Office Administrator	X	X	X		X	X	X	X			X	X		X						X	X	0	X	

Notes: X = Competent; 0 = Under training/to be trained.

Figure 2.2   Standards compared

STANDARDS COMPARED

ISO 9001:2008 is accepted as a world-wide standard for Quality Management systems. "Investors in People" was developed as the British National Standard and is also applied elsewhere. It built on the systems approaches to training pioneered by some Training Boards, particularly Food, Drink and Tobacco I.T.B. Both help in the achievement of tangible and positive business benefits. Both encourage more pro-active planning and clearer business objectives and ensure that staff have the skills required to achieve them. When developed together impact is greatly enhanced.

Basic principles of the standards are:

	ISO 9001:2008	**Investors in People**
Commitment	Commitment to a quality Policy signed by the chief Executive and genuinely reflecting the attitude of top management. The message understood at all levels.	Public commitment from the top to develop all employees to achieve business objectives.
	Quality plans and objectives defined.	
Planning	Regular management review of the quality management system in all areas and assessment of "non-conformance's" against the standard including training. Documented plans for "corrective and preventative action".	Regular reviews of the training and development needs of all employees. Assessment of "gaps" between the standard and performances and the preparation of plans to correct unsatisfactory situations.
Action	Those responsible: • record and identify problems • prevent re-occurrence • pursue solutions • check solutions • control further work until correction • measure results	Taking action to train and develop individuals on recruitment and throughout their employment.
	People trained in monitoring Training needs analysed Records maintained Documents controlled Clear control procedures Systemic procedures for relations with customers and suppliers Human Resource systems in place	Records maintained Documents controlled Clear procedures and instructions
Evaluation	A comprehensive system of internal audits. Regular monitoring, testing and inspection. On-going evaluation of performance and a policy of continuing improvement. Monitoring and measurement.	Evaluation of the investment in training and development, to assess achivement and improve effectiveness.
Third Party Assessment	Audit by an accredited body and issue of a certificate.	Assessment and presentation to a Recognition Panel, Certification as an Investor in People.

ACTION

Assess Human Resource Management Systems as part of ISO 9001:2008!

Appendix 2a: Managing through ISO 9001:2008

Contrary to many common assumptions and beliefs, ISO 9000 is not an old-fashioned 'quality' standard. Regrettably, it is still possible to live in the world of Standards as they were before 9000, but the current standard does represent a conceptual breakthrough.

It is in line with modern management thinking and practice. It is a basis for practical success. It does not require shelves of procedures; it is about producing quality products and services which meet customers' needs and expectations and which can be seen as value for money in the market. It involves selling and delivery as well as 'production and service'.

It is awarded when you are able to demonstrate that you are in control of all the processes which determine the acceptability of your product or service. This means being successful in an organised way and being likely to continue in that way. It implies good management, good selection and good training.

Appendix 2b: Investors in People

In order to be registered as an 'Investor in People' an organisation has to satisfy various requirements by giving evidence to an assessor. This person will look at appropriate documents and interview various people to ensure the requirements are being met.

These 'indicators' are:

- A strategy for improving the performance of the organisation is clearly defined and understood.

- Learning and development is planned to achieve the organisation's objectives.

- Strategies for managing people are designed to promote equality of opportunity in the development of the organisation's people.

- The capabilities managers need to lead, manage and develop people effectively are clearly defined and understood.

- Managers are effective in leading, managing and developing people.

- People's contribution to the organisation is valued and recognised.

- People are encouraged to take ownership and responsibility by being involved in decision making.

- People learn and develop effectively.

- Investment in people improves the performance of the organisation.

- Improvements are continually made to the way people are managed and developed.

3

Who Has to be Trained and When?

A process machine has broken down several times. The production managers are increasingly concerned about losses. Engineers are blamed and immediately called in. They rectify the situation but accuse the operators of mishandling the machine. The operators have had little training but say they could now tell the fitters how to correct or anticipate certain faults if only they had an opportunity to contribute their ideas. They are prevented by the line organisation.

Starting Point in a Specific Training Situation

This brief statement of a situation typical of many industries, illustrates the difficulties of knowing where to start and the possible dangers of starting in the wrong place. What are the training problems?

OPERATOR TRAINING PROBLEM

There is obviously an operator training problem but further analysis is required to establish its significance in the whole situation. There may be significant cues which the operators are missing, manipulative skills which they lack or basic lack of knowledge stemming from poor initial instruction. If so, these must be put right.

However, it is important not only to look at the operators' job on its own, but to consider the links with others. The real breakdown may be at the 'output' rather than the 'input' stage. Whatever happens, the operator side must never be seen in isolation. The trainer must always look at the total situation to get the right answer.

FITTER TRAINING PROBLEM

Although it may require a broader approach, a similar analysis must also be made of the fitters' job. They may have a high level of general skill but lack knowledge of this particular machine. They may know more about the structure of machines than systematic fault-finding. They may be more ready to blame operators and production managers than to seek essential cues from them. An agreed training programme or changes in procedure may emerge from a joint discussion and analysis of the problem.

MANAGEMENT TRAINING PROBLEM

Why had the training situation and its implications not been analysed before? Do all levels of management have or need a full knowledge of the machines and operators concerned? It is likely that most managers will have a number of things to learn from the situation. The trainer has to consider how to arrange for managers to learn without seeming to tell experienced people their job. Although one of the more difficult parts of the operation, this may be the real priority area, as so much often depends on real success in improving understanding and changing attitudes at this level.

GROUP TRAINING PROBLEM

Although it is possible to isolate the individual and sectional requirements in this situation, as in so many training problems, much of the improvement is dependent on group learning. It is possible to summarise certain guiding principles from this illustration:

- From the first, the approach must be a broad one recognising the proper links between groups and sections.

- An easily identifiable and acceptable operator training problem may provide the focus and platform for later development.

- The involvement and learning of managers and other groups may be facilitated by participation in the analysis and training at junior levels.

- The same process and means of involvement is likely to contribute to a recognition and solution of the group problems and ultimately organisational problems, namely:

a) Problems of relationships and integration between levels and groups. These can form barriers to the increase of understanding of the situation and to the development and spread of basic knowledge and skill. They may be exaggerated by formal group ties, such as trade unions. The trainer must consider how learning is affected by status, groupings, facility for group control, job definitions and objectives (written or assumed).

b) Custom and practice problems. These may be related to an earlier environment possibly of a different size using different machinery. They may be one of the key 'anti-learning' factors at the present time.

ORGANISATIONAL DEVELOPMENT PROBLEM

Related to all the previous problems may be an overriding organisational development problem. The basic organisation in the area – production and engineering hierarchies and so on – may inhibit adaptation to deal with the development of skill. Although hardly ever a priority, it may be necessary to consider means of encouraging the organisation to recognise ways of adapting itself to the accelerated development of learning and other problems related to rapid change. Learning and effective training may in the long run be dependent upon a successful 'change system' spread into the organisation. With others, trainers must recognise their role as a 'change agent'.

Methods of Analysing Organisational Problems

The traditional approach to training analysis is by asking questions, of the person and their supervisor. This approach relies on a considerable amount of self-diagnosis; individuals are asked what their training needs are. It is backed by the view that people should know what they want and that the aim of trainers is to provide the opportunity of getting it, probably for themselves. Training is seen essentially as a learning rather than a teaching process. Self-motivation is, of course, a very important factor but self-diagnosis, although having its place, also has its drawbacks. All analysis in the training field must have a large subjective element but to ask training questions of the non-trainer frequently combines subjectivity and superficiality. In spite of these dangers this approach is straightforward and will always form a part of training routines.

Figure 3.1   Supervisory questionnaire

QUESTION

What additional information and training ought you, in your view, receive to do your job satisfactorily?

NAME OF DEPARTMENT	REQUIREMENTS
Quality control	Work measurement standards Bacteriology Statistical analysis Planning procedure Supervisory skills Technical courses Industrial relations
Production	Technical information and knowledge Work standards and measurement techniques Trade unions Visits to other sites Industrial relations Costing Incentive schemes Experience of other departments Ergonomics
Engineering	Fault diagnosis Systematic training of operatives Supervisor training Visits to suppliers of machinery for instruction and to see equipment in assembly Network analyses Programming Stock control

Asking the Person Involved

Response to direct questions of this kind and the advantages and weaknesses involved are best illustrated by example. Figure 3.1 sets out answers to a questionnaire concerned with supervisory responsibilities. Two major themes can be seen in these answers. There is naturally a substantial bias towards self-improvement, not always within the context of the company work arrangements. Answers falling within the work context tend to lack depth mainly because of the inevitably limited perspective and frame of reference of those concerned.

A common fault, unless questions are carefully formed, is that individuals do not really state their own needs but answer according to their assessment of the wishes of management or the requirements of other people. There have been instances of employees merely listing the subjects from courses which they have already attended. Answers may in some cases be more valuable as a general attitude survey than as a training analysis. Many known training problems may be reflected in responses which are totally negative from a training point of view. This information should not be overlooked although the trainer should not be diverted by it.

Asking the Boss

In some situations that dangerously misrepresented phrase 'training is the line manager's responsibility' is common. In many cases the responsibility is formalised as part of the reporting system, see Figure 3.2. Some of the weaknesses are illustrated by the replies from various levels within an organisation. Principal difficulties are that:

- answers are too general;

- experience and training are confused;

- questions can be easily avoided;

- answers are often symptoms of other problems;

- the longer the time span, the more vague and useless the answers.

Better answers can usually be obtained when questions refer directly to knowledge and skills rather than to 'training' concepts of which there are as many and diverse as the bosses involved. There is still the danger that the approach can encourage the boss to look for weaknesses, rather than strengths which can be developed.

Unless an enormous effort is put into the training of managers to appraise and interpret appraisal in training terms there will always be severe limitations to this approach. The best and most economical policy is probably to recognise these limitations and ensure that the trainers involved in interpretation are sufficiently skilled to act both as analysts and as developers of the managers they are working with.

Figure 3.2   Managers' formal assessment of training requirements

QUESTION

What aspects of knowledge and skill should be improved to:

1. Benefit efficiency in meeting the objectives of the present job?
2. Prepare for the next job?

SAMPLE ANSWERS *(a)*
Could well benefit from some extended training in sales forecasting and in computer applications.
Proven experience in a field supervisory position in all its aspects.
Familiarisation with computer techniques. Practical experience of factory distribution operations.
Management training. Personnel relations.
The progressive gaining of technical knowledge and general management training.
Further experience and increased responsibility within the department.
Must quickly learn those few areas of the section with which not fully conversant with.
Method Study and Analytical Appraisal Techniques.
Has a place on a Systems Analysis course but this may only go part way.
Greater knowledge of capital budgets and capital proposals.
Present knowledge is adequate.
Would benefit from more knowledge of printing processes which could help to take decisions
     when called upon to do so by print buyers.
An increased appreciation of continuous audit techniques would always help to contribute to the
     company's conclusions from research in these fields.
Knowledge and skill adequate for present job.
Management course.
Visit to USA.
Concern management courses.
Further knowledge of trade union structure and affairs.
To be aware of the workings of produce management, and so be able to make reasonable requests.
Further technical improvement will automatically come with policy lines set from research and
     experience. Management is improved and delegates more, but could probably improve on
     explaining details of operations by fuller communication at each phase of exercise with those
     members of staff who are slower or less able to grasp broad outline.
Experience within the department together with the opportunity from time to time to attend
     management courses.
Further experience and increased responsibility within the department.
General management communication.
More background knowledge of the catering industry, particularly in London.
Computer programming course.

SAMPLE ANSWERS *(b)*
Management course, and computer course would help.
I do not see him moving to another field.
A course in general management would be of benefit.
Familiarisation with computer systems, systems analysis and programming techniques.
Further experience and increased responsibility within the department.
Any general training course to widen knowledge of the business would help.
Practice in larger-scale transport planning.
Knowledge of cold storage work elsewhere.
Industrial relations.
General administration.

Operational Analysis

The main subject of training analysis is not individuals or their bosses but the operation. Training is of value rather than interest only when it contributes to a more profitable and effective operation. Questions about the real purpose of training cannot be asked too often. Training for the sake of particular individuals or groups or, worse still, for its own sake, only militates against the main purpose of training for the sake of the operation and for the sake of profit.

Trainers are in no way different from any other industrial specialist. They must know the real work problems whether these are in terms of sales, production, human relations, or anything else. The essential and primary skill of the trainer is in interpreting these problems in training terms. Learning aspects of the problems must be recognised and described before teaching or training remedies can be considered.

There are two major dangers in this area. Either remedies are prescribed because they seem attractive in themselves or are the trainers' 'stock in trade' or remedies are prescribed for problems which could better be solved in other ways, simply because they have been uncovered and defined during the training analysis. An important training skill is to know when not to interfere – when not to train. If problems are essentially ones of administration, method study or other areas, they should be recognised as such. The trainer's role may be limited to that of a pure catalyst. Once the problem has been recognised, no further prompting or organised training may be necessary. Seeking the problem to fit the remedy can only lead to extensive waste in other ways like sending people on training courses because they are in vogue or seeking a Standard because it is in fashion. Ironically, Investors in People may be the wrong investment in the wrong people. The tendency is often to go for the impressive and sophisticated, but if learning will, for instance, be improved simply by a better flow of information this is all that is required. If people can read the right books there may be no need for sophisticated programmes. If operational problems are really examined in detail, true training problems are always likely to be plentiful enough.

The operational approach not only enables the trainer to keep his feet on the ground but it gives better opportunity for seeing key problems, the symptoms of which may appear in various forms in different areas of an organisation. The process is situational analysis rather than job analysis. The training of individuals and groups can then be linked in a more appropriate manner. It is also easier to recognise where the learning problems are those essentially related to a group rather than an individual and these are the very problems which either individuals or their bosses in isolation find very difficult to recognise.

Independent Job Analysis

Once a general questioning approach has indicated the appropriate training areas in terms of performance and cost, the trainer will usually require a detailed analysis of the job itself or of a group of jobs in order to find out what is involved in successful performance. It may be possible, particularly at operative level, to obtain this job analysis from a work study specialist, although it must be recognised that this can usually be used as a basis only for a skill and training analysis. A study produced purely to describe what is being done in a particular timescale may not give enough information about how the job is expected to be performed. At operative level it may be necessary to amass more movement and sensory data, as in the skills analysis sheet illustrated in Figure 6.2 (see Chapter 6). An illustration of the use of more basic data, such as MTM[1] data for an early and very economical analysis is given in Chapter 6. At the management level the trainer will sometimes need to know more about the style required than the usual job description will provide. Whatever the approach, the job analysis must be kept in perspective. The first stage must always be to analyse the total situation and see which areas are to be given priority in further probing. Unless the broad picture and overall objectives are clear, much time and effort will be wasted on unnecessary and redundant analysis. The real problem may be to learn to do without certain jobs or at least change them. Premature analysis here is futile.

What Standards are Expected?

When all the preparatory analysis has been carried out it is not uncommon to find a trainer hopelessly frustrated by lack of basic performance data indicating what is expected and certainly what is possible. This is often a principal reason for starting in the area where at least some of this information is normally

---

1   MTM refers to methods-time measurement which is a predetermined time system developed at the Methods Engineering Council, Pittsburgh, Pennsylvania, USA by Maynard, Stegemerten and Schwab. The background to the system is described in their book, *Methods-Time Measurement*. Predetermined time systems are based on the fact that the time required to perform the same motion varies rarely between workers who have had adequate practice.

readily available – at the basic task level; at the operator level. Even if some basic work has not been done, it is usually possible to establish basic criteria quite quickly.

What are the Sources of Control Data?

Many of the basic sources of control data have already been referred to earlier but it is worth summarising the possibilities. The following is a checklist which is suggested as a general guide:

- Basic method study and production control data (including engineering measurement).

- Synthetic data, for example MTM.

- Overall performance targets.

- Training target times and checklist developed by the trainer.

- Planning and accounting data.

- Individual and group appraisal systems.

- Comparative data from similar operations.

- Traditional standards.

- Data correlating methods and work performance, for example on-the-job follow-up in the operator training situation.

- ERGOM (European Research Group on Management) research follow-up in the management area.

- 'Management by objectives' standards and targets.

- Key performance indicators (KPIs).

The use of various types of control data under these headings will be considered in detail in later chapters. They are the key to a true systems approach to training.

However, it is surprising how frequently apparently sophisticated organisations lack basic measurement information or have it in a form which only relates to a specialised incentive payment application. A first training priority is to ensure that the best possible control data are prepared. This normally involves some adjustment and even basic training outside the main operational area for those concerned with statistical control. The emphasis on Measurement, Analysis and Improvement in ISO 9001:2008 is an example of this. The fact is that

MEASUREMENT + ANALYSIS AND TRAINING = IMPROVEMENT.

It is still very unusual for a trainer to come into a situation where the standard information gives a guide not only to what is expected but to what should be expected. Usually, trainers develop personal targets as they proceed which may or may not be related to previous standards. The use of certain highly developed synthetic data, such as MTM can be a great help in this respect and a review of this is given in the case study in Chapter 6. Outside the operating area the setting of standards with any precision is even less common. Certain general engineering applications are developing steadily but for supervisors and management, appraisal of performance is usually either strictly limited to the minimum salary requirements or surrounded by pseudo-scientific but basically subjective character assessment. This makes it inevitable and essential that training is considered from the start in a very broad context, recognising the necessity of influencing objective setting approaches and management standards setting through the processes of staff appraisal and organisational development. Without these, management training can be an educationalist's paradise and a trainer's nightmare. Exercises are carried out because they seem to be good in themselves rather than to achieve any particular goal or target – 'fancy courses'. Some see training as good in itself whereas by itself it can be expensive and useless. Standards should consider the value and purpose of training and not give 'brownie points' just for its existence. Training provided by Standards bodies is not always the best example of the art.

4

Understanding Learning Problems

There will always be a variety of learning issues in most operational problems making it very difficult to establish any simple set of guidelines, but there are a number of major categories which can usefully be considered.

Lack of Knowledge and Skill

If performance is being hampered by an obvious lack of knowledge and skill, this is normally relatively easy to recognise and, although the training remedies may need to be at various levels of sophistication, there should be no fundamental problems once the objectives of a particular course or training activity have been defined. This is the area in which training is most closely associated with the traditional educational process and where most needs are normally recognised, as illustrated by the questionnaires which have already been discussed. In the later chapters the range of approaches will be examined in detail.

Knowledge and Skill Not Being Applied

Problems which are frequently seen as being related to lack of knowledge may in many instances be something entirely different. For instance, there are many programmes of induction, safety and quality training where very effective teaching is offered in the knowledge and skill required without a clear impact on results. The reaction is normally to halt or intensify the basic teaching operation and it may be some time before the whole process is seen as being futile or, in some cases, perhaps destructive.

There may well be contradictions in the organisation which may lead to many problems, frequently defined as attitude problems. Operators may be taught to use machinery bearing in mind all the necessary safety precautions, whereas the organisation rewards them entirely on the basis of output. A carefully prepared learning pattern is, therefore, changed to meet the obvious requirements of managers and the standards these imply.

In other instances, the training scheme may be designed to produce excellent results in an atmosphere of friendly and highly participative management when the basic management style trainees will eventually have to work in is strongly authoritarian and/or 'unfriendly'. On transfer from the training situation to the real operational situation, skills which were thought to have been learned can disappear overnight as the atmosphere changes.

In all these cases, the basic teaching skill is, of course, important, but unless the programme is related to the learning and motivation of the real work environment, unless operators learn to accept the working situation as well as gain a skill, results can be very disturbing.

'Anti-Learning' Factors

Most operational situations contain a number of elements which will restrict the development of learning regardless of the methods employed. A range of these will be discussed later. They may vary from the basic conflict situation on the shop floor, which can give rise to clearly recognised restrictive practices, to the limitations of the 'rat race' in the management area.

Learning Theory

Learning theory has developed rapidly in the last century. This development has taken a number of directions and there are still some basic disagreements amongst theorists. There is, however, sufficient common ground for the trainer to recognise a number of useful generalisations which have a high degree of reliability and validity. This can provide the basis for some clearly defined principles of learning which can be examined against the background of any training situation.

Although there are many definitions of learning, it is probably sufficient to recognise that we are concerned essentially with learning as a relatively permanent change in behaviour that occurs as a result of practice and experience. Behind the process of learning, in spite of variations of theory, one can recognise the four basic concepts of: Drive, Stimulus, Response and Reinforcement. Amongst the main learning theories, four basic approaches can be seen.

BEHAVIOURAL APPROACH

The basis of learning is by trial and error, repetition being particularly important. This is the most rudimentary form of learning. A stimulus is followed by a random attempt to receive a reward or avoid punishment. Actions which are rewarded are reinforced and vice versa.

GESTALT APPROACH

The basis of learning is seen as insight. The total situation is seen as a meaningful pattern. A number of stimuli and responses producing rewards and punishments are perceived as a whole. This type of learning is particularly associated with the learning of ideas rather than a mass of detailed material.

MODEL APPROACH

Learning may be achieved by avoiding the failures of someone who has learned basically by trial and error. Behaviour is essentially that of modelling the behaviour of others. This type of learning is particularly useful when applied to physical skills, although a certain amount of trial and error is almost always necessary. Models of behaviour set by managers are particularly powerful. Genuine recognition of people and their contributions is at the heart of leadership.

INSTRUCTION

Learning is dependent on communication from others who are more knowledgeable about situations. Instruction is, of course, entirely dependent on the learner knowing the language of instruction whether this is in the form of words or symbols. All four of these learning approaches may be illustrated quite easily in a number of training situations in industry. Although instruction may be the main process, some arrangement will normally be made for perceptual organisation and modelling by demonstration as well as a period of practice in which controlled trial and error takes place. Of increasing significance is the role of the trainer in stimulating learning by creating situations which produce new insights. A number of writers have looked in considerable detail at the background theories relevant to industrial training, particularly Bass and Vaughan in *Training in Industry – The Management of Learning* (Bass and Vaughan, 1967). The important aspects for the trainer are the recognition of the basic learning principles which can be drawn from the background theories and psychology.

Transfer

The central problem of training, as opposed to general education, is to ensure that the basic stimulus-response situations facilitate an adequate transfer of learning to the operational situation. In many ways, traditional on-the-job training, although criticised, has clear and obvious advantages in this respect sometimes overlooked by educational theorists. There is no conflict between the techniques and motivators used in the training period and those in the following industrial situation. In terms of skill, knowledge, attitude and personal relationships, there are excellent opportunities for the creation of a continuous development process. The main danger is often in the modelling aspect of learning. So much depends on the characteristics of the on-the-job trainer and the ability to create adequate learning situations. In fact, although it is possible in theory to create excellent conditions for learning on-the-job, in practice it is extremely difficult, primarily because of the difficulty of ensuring control of the learning process and its adequate continuation in a situation where production rather than training is the prime consideration. These control and organisational problems usually make it necessary to engage in some training on-the-job with all the attendant risks in terms of inadequate transfer of learning.

At the operator training level, there are, of course, many instances where a quite successful compromise is reached with training being carried out adjacent to the main operation rather than completely separate from it, with the result that environmental situations do not change radically at the end of the formal training period. A number of instances can be quoted of situations where learning of this kind has been more effective than either quite well controlled on-the-job training or highly formalised teaching away from the job.

The fish filleting training outlined in Chapter 6 was first started in a training room completely away from the operation. Later trials made it clear that the pace of work developed more effectively when the training group was on a line within the main production building alongside skilled operatives working at high speed.

Practice and Repetition

On-the-job training again often has some advantages in being able to provide possibilities for more practice and repetition, in some cases the only possibilities for real practice. However, the theoretical advantages of completely integrated training are often outweighed by the difficulties of organising it and the difficulties of control lead one to certain types of systematic training off-the-job. Here practice and repetition may be in fact better organised in learning terms because of the ability to arrange the sequence of teaching to take advantage of the division of the job into parts where this is appropriate and by distributing practice. Experimental studies have shown that, on the whole, distributed practice is superior to 'massed practice' and that, in certain age groups, part learning and learning by stages have distinct advantages. In general, the whole method is said to be better:

- with highly intelligent people;

- with distributed practice;

- when the material is relatively short and meaningful;

- with older workers.

Reinforcement

Although, again in theory, it is possible to provide adequate reinforcement of learning in an on-the-job situation, it is in relation to this aspect of learning that many of the greater dangers occur. Major reasons for inadequate learning on-the-job are lack of reinforcement or reinforcement of wrong practices. For instance, a working situation at the operative level may encourage workers to work too quickly in the early stages at the expense of failure to establish certain basic performance habits which are crucial to higher-level performance and learning at later stages.

Willingness to Change

The attitude to training and the changes this implies are a very important factor in the learning situation although frequently underestimated. In this connection, on-the-job training, in spite of its many other theoretical advantages, has many shortcomings. The creation of the right environment to encourage people to want to learn is entirely dependent on the person doing the training and if, as in many cases, their main job is not to train but to do a job themselves, they are probably unlikely to be very helpful. Difficulties also arise, however, in many of the more formal approaches to training even where the learning issues involved are very carefully organised as in the case of programmed learning and computer-based instruction. Areas in which this aspect of learning seems to be best encouraged are those where there is a high degree of participation and discussion. This applies not only at supervisory and management levels, but also in operator training. The dialogue between the trainer and an operative is of crucial importance not only in setting out the basic training requirements but in creating the atmosphere of encouragement. Although the establishment of rapport is usually mentioned at the beginning of any training programme, its real importance to instructors is not always sufficiently stressed. It is seen as merely creating a pleasant social setting rather than having a fundamental influence on learning.

Participation

The main contribution of participation to the learning situation, as has already been mentioned, is in influencing the development of positive attitudes. In this the quality of participation is important, and although it is an inevitable element of most on-the-job training, real involvement may be limited and can best be obtained in an organised off-the-job discussion. Learning encouraged in this way is also particularly important in the development of concepts as opposed to detailed knowledge. In this respect, the lecture has obvious shortcomings and in some areas is quite rightly replaced by discussion or case study techniques.

Knowledge of Results

This aspect of learning has been stressed in most training programmes and studies of training for a long time. It is clearly an integral part of any organised operator training. More important, it is now being recognised as a part of the learning situation for managers and for the whole management team with the development of objective setting and more objective reporting. The importance of accurate feedback in management development is receiving steadily increasing attention. Training evaluation is now seen as a process of continuous feedback rather than a beginning or end point measurement. The principles involved can be extended on a systematic basis still further by focusing attention on the learning process of groups as a result of more objective analysis of progress. It is interesting that, while steady improvements have been made in obtaining better learning curves for individuals, often on fairly simple operations, as a result of providing better knowledge results, more senior management groups have often maintained consistent patterns of behaviour, for instance, in making a series of financial and organisational decisions. In these areas, although there is at first sight more control data, this is not always used to improve the learning of the group as a whole so that decision patterns themselves are steadily improved. In analysing training problems for a large part of an organisation, a useful place to start is the consideration of the pattern of major decision taking to see whether there is evidence of improvement and learning from generally recognised mistakes.

One of the biggest dangers is the concealment of mistakes and fundamental errors. Banking is an unfortunate example of this. Lone operators hiding their mistakes can lead to the collapse of whole organisations. One of the most powerful ways of avoiding this is by developing and training groups of internal auditors who are not inspectors but colleagues and team leaders who can look for both corrective and preventive action. ISO 2001:2008 provides an excellent basis for developing this type of constructive learning in an organisation.

Self-Motivation

One of the arguments for on-the-job training is that much learning can be very satisfactorily achieved if people are left to themselves and that in fact the major contribution to learning will be as a result of self-development. There is some truth in this but it is important to recognise that, in many cases, effective motivation will need a trigger. This may be provided by formal off-the-job training or may be an integral part of systematic on-the-job training. In the management area, the process can be encouraged without going far from the job situation by techniques such as mutual goal setting.

Figure 4.1 illustrates a conventional objective-setting approach applied in the training area. Many companies have now had experience of this type of definition acting as a very useful starting point for a change and improvement in performance.

Once agreed with the boss, the annual objectives and measurements in columns three and four can provide a manager with a self-development programme, which is entirely linked with the objectives of the team and the organisation. Although this is a self-improvement process, there are still controls. The definition of objectives has acted as a trigger for systematic improvement within the job.

This particular illustration was produced a few years ago as a supplement to the job descriptions of training officers in organisations of between 1,000 and 2,500 people.

General Departmental Functions

The development and maintenance of an adequate and appropriate training organisation, providing effective systems for diagnosing and dealing with training needs and focusing the use of training resources on the most profitable areas.

Figure 4.1   Objective setting for a training and development manager – sample document

MANAGER'S OBJECTIVES	OBJECTIVES (YEAR)	MEASUREMENT
Organisation		
To ensure that the training is appropriate to the organisation requirements and that sufficient training specialists are available for analysis and instruction.	The appointment and training of an operator training supervisor. The retraining of instructors. The instruction of work study engineers in skills analysis.	Numbers recruited and trained. How far are key training requirements being met – is training being organised in all 'high pay-off areas'?
Management development and training		
Systematic identification of 'talent'. Integrated individual training through 'development groups' etc. The recognition of 'staging-post' positions. The systematic definition of management objectives and allied training. Systematic introductory training for all jobs. The organisation of appropriate courses required to supplement integrated training.	The definition of objectives and training requirements for all supervisory jobs. Review of appraisal systems. Clear definitions of job knowledge requirements prior to all appointments. The organisation of courses in special techniques- maintenance, engineering, statistics, network analysis.	Have effective systems been developed? What evidence is there of their success? Are training needs reviewed regularly with departmental heads? Have recruitment requirements been anticipated? Percentage of outside recruitment necessary. Has adequate introductory training been completed? Have courses been completed? Have they been evaluated?
Operator training		
The establishment of a system providing for skills analysis and instruction, and the measurement and targeting of performance. The establishment of a training cost control system designed to control expenditure and indicate savings. The establishment of relationships with line managers at all levels which enable the training schemes to operate through production departmental management.	The definition of high pay-off areas. The focusing of analysis, instruction and performance measurement resources on these areas. The establishment of training schemes in areas which will indicate the possible scope of further training developments, i.e. the selection of a representative sample of jobs. The appointment and training of additional instructors and auditors.	Is introductory training always carried out? Have instructors been available when required? Is the system successful in terms of: 1 Improved performance? 2 Reduced costs? 3 Improved yield and quality? 4 Other objective measures, e.g. turnover etc.

Figure 4.1   Continued

MANAGER'S OBJECTIVES	OBJECTIVES (YEAR)	MEASUREMENT
Craft training		
The application of skills analysis and systematic instruction to craftsmen and apprentices.	The completion of skills analysis in key areas, e.g. packaging fitting. The provision of special information courses concerned with key technical developments. The establishment of tests of performance for first-year apprentices. The application of programmed learning techniques in agreed areas.	Have skills analyses been carried out? Have these formed the basis for training? What performance tests have been introduced?
Education		
Optimum use of a company education scheme for employees who will benefit in their jobs by attending courses. Influencing local education institutions in running courses which are relevant to the Company needs.	An increase of 25% in courses involving day release or full-time study. The provision of adequate first year apprentice training in local colleges.	College attendance records. Are apprentice training facilities available?
Training development		
The application of some training resources to the development of new training techniques and training required for new machinery and production requirements.	The validation of programmed learning techniques for apprentices. The establishment of controlled inspection of training exercises.	What has been done?
Job knowledge		
To keep abreast of new developments in the training field with special reference to: 1 new legislation; 2 new methods and techniques.		Is training geared to legislative requirements? Are new methods and techniques being applied?
Training environment		
To ensure that training aims and training potential are understood by management. The maintenance of relationships with management which enable the trainer to operate effectively.	The systematic publication and circulation of training results.	Is the role of the training department understood? Is the trainer integrated with the management group? Are relationships with key departments, e.g. method, study, good? Are training activities willingly assimilated into departmental work?

5

Techniques of Establishing Training Needs

The discussion of the recognition of training needs has so far been general, although a number of specific techniques have been referred to as part of the total situation. Many approaches are well known and their nature and purpose self-evident. At this stage, therefore, they will only be listed for summary purposes while some others slightly less usual or technically interesting will be covered in more detail.

Observation

Observation almost seems too obvious to mention, but it is a most essential part of the process and is often underestimated. Much stress is usually laid in detailed interview appraisal and so on, but acute personal observation can often add those indications of knack and key aspects of the learning system which are vital from the training point of view. It is important to remember that those familiar with the situations are conditioned to expect certain things to happen and even trained observers such as Method Study Engineers, may only see the process from their own special point of view. It is always essential to spend a significant period in the early stages in personal observation looking particularly for:

- the links in the learning system;

- key ones which are not used for learning purposes;

- assumptions about the learning situation;

- key performance elements.

Planned Interviews

The planning of a series of interviews with all concerned with the problem situation is at the heart of any systematic approach to training needs analysis. The fact that they are planned, however, does not mean that they should be obviously planned. As in selection interviewing, it is essential to establish a sound personal relationship with the interviewee and clumsy over-formalised approaches can, of course, inhibit this.

The important thing is to know what is really wanted, covering key categories of information. For this an outline five-point plan can be valuable, similar to that used for selection purposes, as follows:

1.   *First impression.* The particular situation and its relation to learning problems. First indications of skill level and the nature of the learning problem. Characteristics of the individual or group concerned.

2.   *Associated problems.* The individual's view of links with other training problems and broader operational and organisation questions.

3.   *Trainee view.* The trainee's view of learning problems, if any.

4.   *Trainer view.* The trainer's view of problems as a trainer, and the role to be played in improving the learning situation.

5.   *Operational view.* The job as seen by those involved, its purpose, structure, standards, controls and so on.

As a general guide to an assessment of the total training need, the trainer may rate this on a rough 'training needs scale'.

Each rough rating will only have any significance in itself but the total profile of scores will be of particular interest to the trainer and give some basis of comparison between various individuals viewing the problem from different angles. Relative differences between the trainee view and the trainer view may be of particular interest. An approach to this rating system is given in Figure 5.1.

Figure 5.1   Outline plan for training needs analysis

Score	1	2	3	4	5
First Impression	Low skill level. Learning problems ones of basic knowledge. Limited pay-off indicated. Problems well understood.	Limited skill. Mainly general knowledge problems. Some payoff indicated. Problems generally well understood.	Average skill. Mixture of skill and knowledge problems. Good payoff indicated. Problems generally well understood.	Considerable skill and knowledge problems. Evidence of other learning problems. Probably good pay-off. Problems hardly understood. Managers involved in the learning process.	High skill level. Extensive knowledge required. Other major learning problems. High long-term pay-off. Problem not properly understood.
Associated problems	An isolated problem. No wider implications.	Some links with other areas. Well understood.	A broad training problem, but one which can be tackled with a good general training approach.	Some links with other jobs frustrating learning in the area.	Links with other areas confuse the learning situation. Much broader organisation problem probably the major consideration.
The trainee view	No major learning problems. Those present easily recognisable.	Few learning problems, well recognised.	Some clear skill and knowledge problems presenting training difficulties but well recognised.	Extensive skill and knowledge problems and associated problems well recognised.	Extensive problems little understood.
The trainer view	No major learning problems. Those present easily recognisable.	Few learning problems, well recognised.	Some clear skill and knowledge problems presenting training difficulties but well recognised.	Extensive skill and knowledge problems and associated problems well recognised.	Extensive problems little understood.
The operational view	Simple job clearly understood.	More complex job but clearly understood. Clear objectives. Well established and recognisable controls.	More complex job. Structure partially understood. Generally clear objectives but limited objective standards and control.	Complex job. Partially understood. Vague objectives and limited controls. High cost levels – savings likely.	Complex job integrated with others. System not understood. Vague objectives. Subjective controls. Significant and expensive operations – good savings likely.

Appraisal Procedures

Without some form of appraisal procedure, training at management level is carried out in a vacuum. Appraisal is essential for the setting of targets and standards and can be used at the same time as a vehicle for posing direct training questions. Standard types of formal approach and responses have been discussed in Chapter 3. The trainer must try to ensure that adequate appraisal is being carried out but should preferably not be directly involved in it. There are dangers in the trainer being associated with the personal assessment and measurement of performance for payment purposes. Trainees will feel inhibited and present an acceptable facade rather than a true basis for development and training. In addition, involvement in appraisal is time consuming and inevitably takes attention away from key training problems.

Training Review Meetings

Training analysis and preparation is rarely complete without some form of group appraisal of the situation. A formal meeting may, as in other areas of business, be an appropriate way of obtaining this. For this purpose, the meeting should have a clearly defined role in deciding training requirements and a means of executive action. It can then be used by the trainer as a positive means of implementing training proposals rather than merely a sounding board. Advantages of the meeting are:

- a quick consensus view of training needs can be obtained;

- executive action in a number of areas can be quickly authorised;

- it enables managers to learn by discussion of the broad issues involved in training.

The whole process may be seen as part of a 'Management Review Meeting' as required and described in the ISO 9001:2008 Management Standard. There is, however, a danger that there may be too little sound training knowledge in the group, presenting the trainer with a major problem of interpretation and explanation in a far from ideal learning situation. Members will feel the need to say and do things before the trainer has had time to fully explain the learning context. This can lead to the establishment of bad training practice on individual prejudices and inadequate knowledge which can hinder training development for a long period. If there seems any danger of this happening, such meetings should be avoided.

A further danger is that training analysis may be too exclusively focused around the formal meeting at the expense of other approaches.

Attitude Surveys

Attitude surveys are normally cited as one of the tools of training analysis. They can, of course, provide additional depth and perspective but the number of trainers who become involved in this type of operation in the early stages of their activity must be very limited and rightly so. There is little evidence of their being justified in the initial audit. Competent and properly planned conventional interviewing can usually provide more than sufficient information. There is also some danger of obtaining misleading information and becoming involved in many non-training problems.

Activity Sampling

It may be necessary in some instances to obtain further information by direct sampling of the activity. This will normally be the case if there appear to be discrepancies in the information coming from other sources. Sampling of this kind is a time-consuming process and is probably only necessary in more sophisticated work environments, it is not something which should be done because it is fashionable or for its own sake. An example of the type of information which can be obtained is given in Figure 5.2.

Figure 5.2   Activity sampling

ACTIVITY	APPROXIMATE PERCENTAGE OF TIME		
	SUPERVISOR A	SUPERVISOR B	SUPERVISOR C
1. Engineering breakdown fixed personally or with other non-fitters	1.7	0.0	0.9
2. Engineering breakdown fixed by fitters or electricians. Time spent with them	8.6	2.8	9.3
3. Personal needs	5.8	4.0	7.0
4. Social (labour control)	6.4	13.9	15.9
5. Social (administrative)	4.4	16.8	14.0
6. Technical (raw material)	5.9	17.6	21.2
7. Technical (line control)	67.2	44.9	31.7

Diaries

Alongside the process of activity sampling, additional information can more easily be obtained by asking those concerned to keep a diary of their activities. This can give very useful further information about the actual activities concerned and is especially valuable in drawing attention to differences between individuals – carrying out similar jobs in different ways. The keeping of a diary also has the advantage of getting those concerned fully involved in the analysis process and is likely to ensure greater commitment to any subsequent training operation. Examples of the kind of information obtained from diaries are given in Figure 5.3.

Figure 5.3   Supervisor's diary – food processing

TIME:	SECTION: MEAT ACTIVITY/OCCURRENCE	DURATION (MINUTES)	CODE	ANY ADDITIONAL REMARKS
07:45 – 09:00	Read dept. log book, check labour materials etc. ready for line to run	10	7	
	Allocate people to jobs on-line	6	4	
	Dish jams on hooder	12	2	F/mate working on this
	Packing m/c	7	2	Inform fitter
	Slicer breakdown	10	2	Inform fitter
	Patrol line	25	7	Cover all areas
09:00 – 10:00	Clean coat from clothing store	10	3	
	Check packaging supplies on-line	10	6	At request of store F/lift breakdown no supplies out as yet
	Patrol line	30	7	All areas
	No meat on-line	5	6	Progress from prep. room
	Check meat yield	5	6	OK
10:00 – 11:00	Tea break	15		
	No meat on-line	5	6	
	Progressing meat from prep room	40	7	Line running short of meat
11:00 – 12:00	Progressing meat from prep. room	15	7	All morning spend time on slicers to push this along
	Personal needs	10	3	
	Patrol line	25	7	All areas
	Assist operator to change foil	5	1	
	Check meat yield	5	6	OK
12:00 – 13:00	Bonus query	15	5	From female operative
	Patrol line	10	7	All areas
	Meat shortage	5	7	Progress from prep. room
	Attend dispenser	10	7	Run empty for L/break sanitation
	Lunch break	20		

Figure 5.3   Continued

TIME:	SECTION: MEAT ACTIVITY/OCCURRENCE	DURATION (MINUTES)	CODE	ANY ADDITIONAL REMARKS
13:00 – 14:00	Lunch break	10		No stock when line restarted
	Return staff to line from canteen	5	4	
	Progress meat from prep. room	15	7	
	Have empty tank removed and full tank put into position	7	7	
	Progress meat from prep. room	23	7	
14:00 – 15:00	Progress meat from prep. room	60	7	Whole hour spent in prep. room. Operatives having trouble with slicers, meat difficult to slice
15:00 – 16:30	Foil jams on hooder	12	1	Assist to clear
	Breakdown on slicer	5	1	Inform no fitters available
	Tea break	10		
	Collect additional froster tickets from office	4	5	
			6	
	Check supplies available	7		OK
	Patrol line	40	7	Cover all areas
	Take final count	5	7	
	Enter into log book			
	Calculate daily meat yield	5	6	

Note: The code refers to Figure 5.2.

Film Analysis

The use of film and video tape, particularly in the field of operator training, made a significant impact. Although there are important technical and cost differences between the two media, their fundamental contribution to the analysis situation is very similar. The direct advantages are speed and effectiveness.

Despite the time taken to prepare and install the equipment, film or video recording can enable a vast amount of material to be recorded and stored for analysis very quickly. Most of the saving in time is in the observation time on-the-job, which is therefore particularly important in limiting the disruption of production.

As well as being quicker, video will often also contribute to a better job. The data collection process is less fallible and the information can be readily studied away from the operation. If necessary, every frame and every movement can be studied in detail away from the 'hurly-burly' of the production operation. In many cases this will lead to a better recognition of skill, not only because a more thorough study is made of the material but because all those concerned with the operation can observe a playthrough at the same time and contribute their own views about the skills involved.

SUPERVISORY TRAINING

In addition to its main direct advantages, analysis of this kind also has a number of very useful side effects. In particular, by taking some of the analysis away from the job itself it is possible to involve supervisors much more in a recognition of what is happening within the job and the total environment. They can be asked to watch the playback of material and interpret the analysis being made. In this situation it is much easier for them to share the responsibility with training specialists. They can make a fuller and much more realistic contribution to the whole process and as a result will normally have a much more positive attitude to everything that is going on. Apart from the effect on training there is also the indirect effect in that supervisors will in fact, learn much more detail about what is happening within their line which can only be of help to them in terms of direct supervision.

OPERATOR TRAINING

The processes also help in enabling operators as well as supervisors to be involved in *the* process of analysis. They will normally be fascinated to watch their own operations and to comment on what is happening and what is going wrong. This will undoubtedly produce a much more positive attitude to change, stronger motivation and a much greater likelihood of success with any new skill or method. Video tapes which have been produced for analysis can, of course, be used for direct demonstration.

TRAINING DEVELOPMENT

The use of video material in this area has been particularly important. It enables the storage of analytical and teaching material. This is particularly important where operations are intermittent or are transferred from one site to another.

It is important to note that although both film and video tape are sometimes considered to be expensive and require a professional operation, this need not be so. Once the basic camera and recording equipment has been purchased, subsequent costs are often very low and results entirely satisfactory for analysis purposes can be obtained by a trainer with average competence with a camera without expensive professional assistance.

The further development in the context of on-line training is reviewed in Chapter 16.

6

Case Study 1: Training Analysis of a Manual Skill

The purpose of this and the following chapter is to illustrate more specifically the general approaches so far discussed. The range of examples is designed to allow wide general references and implications to be examined from the base of a limited selection of particular situations. Although considerable detail will be given in some areas, the aim is that this should encourage comparison with a range of similar situations and therefore be of general illustrative value to a number of industries and occupations.

Special emphasis will be given to two questions, the recognition of problems and the sequence of the analysis.

The follow up, in terms of the arrangement of training programmes and of wider organisational and business implications, will also be reviewed, not only for the sake of completeness but more importantly to indicate the links with the general development of training analysis in other problem areas.

Most detailed analysis of training needs has been carried out in the operator training field. The literature is full of detailed case studies. Job analysis, method specification, target setting and all the other associated techniques form part of what is now well-established doctrine. The terms 'skills analysis' is generally, although not always precisely, used to describe a whole range of activities from simple TWI[1] courses to extremely abstruse approaches to work appraisal.

The problem in some areas is now too much analysis rather than too little. The essential emphasis of key elements and activities required as the basis for training is sometimes completely lost in a mass of job breakdown material. The result of over-analysis of this kind can be confusion and breakdown of the whole training system.

---

1   TWI – Training Within Industry.

The example used in this chapter, although detailed, illustrates the need for early selectivity in analysis at this level and the establishment of clear training and learning priorities.

Operational Situation

A large food-processing operation initially employing about 60 men to fillet fish by hand experiences a number of training problems with the filleters over a period of about three years. The problems stemmed from:

1.   A need to recruit and train 60 additional filleters quickly.

2.   Inadequacies in previous training and recruitment practices.

Hand filleting is a traditional skill and methods and standards are common to fishing ports where the work has been done in the same way for many centuries.

Several groups of filleters were trained during the three-year period with increasing success in terms of improved performance and training times. Feedback from each exercise contributed to the continuous review of the original analysis and improvements in the training programme.

Figure 6.1a   Job analysis of fish filleting – summary

MTM I/	MTM SUMMARY SHEET			Ref -------------		
Product: *Small plaice*			Factory _____			
Operation: *Crosscut Fillet + trim*			Dept *White fish*			
Equipment: *Knife bench*						
Compiled by: *J Brown*			Date *22/3/09*			
					TOTAL	
El no	Element		TMU	Freq	TMU	Unit
A	*Fillet black side*		228.2	*1*	228.2	*Fish*
B	*Trim 2 pieces from black side + pa*		58.2	*1*	58.2	"
C	*Fillet white side*		259.1	*1*	259.1	"
B	*Trim 2 pieces from white side + pa*		58.2	*1*	58.2	"
				Total TMU's	603.7	
		Conversion Factor *00067* Total 8 Mins			.405	

Figure 6.1b Job analysis of fish filleting – detail

MTM I/E			DETAILED ANALYSIS			Sheet 1 Ref _____
Product *Small plaice*						Operation Crosscut fillet + trim
Description		LH	TMU	RH		Description
Black side						
Reach to whole fish		*R12B*	12.9			
Grasp head		*GIA*	2.0			
To block		*MIOB*	12.2	*(M6C)*		*Knife to fish*
			11.8	*M8C*		*Cut round and cut*
			4.6	*M2B*		*Knife point to neck*
			16.2	*P2SE*		
			8.0	*M4C*		*Insert blade (flat) into fish*
			2.0	*MEB*		*Turn blade*
			13.5	*MIOC*		*Cut from neck along back*
						bone half way to tail
			5.7	*M3B*		*Move back knife*
Pull fish to LHS to resist		*(M68)*	10.6	*APT*		
cutting						
			7.1	*M6Cm*		*Cut to tail + cut*
			7.2	*mM88*		*Continue cutting stroke*
To cut fillet		*(R28)*				
		(GIA)	10.3	*MGC*		*Knife to tail*
				T602		
Pull open fillet for		*MIOB*	12.2			
cutting						
			11.8	*M8C*		*Cut from tail to head*
						(half way)
		G2	5.6	*(M48)*		*Back for second stroke*
		(M68)	11.8	*M8C*		*Continue cut from tail to*
						Head off
			11.8	*M8C*		*Knife to neck*
			16.2	*P2SE*		
			11.8	*M8C*		*Cut from head to tail*
						(half way). (Separating
						top fillet from b-bone)
			6.9	*M48*		*Back for 2nd stroke*
			10.6	*AP2*		
Pull fillet open		*(M28)*	5.4	*M4Cm*		*Cut to tail + off*
Total TMU's 225.2						

Note: Document shows start of analysis only.

Development of the Analysis: Stage 1

ANALYSIS OF MATERIAL

The method of filleting was prescribed by the method study department in the business. It was designed to give a better yield than was generally achieved in the district. 'Experienced' workers elsewhere usually had little incentive to cut the maximum flesh from the fish as the customer had already paid for the whole fish. This business, however, prepared fillets for sale by weight and so yield was of paramount importance. The type of method analysis provided is shown in Figure 6.1.

ANALYSIS OF SKILL

Using the method study analysis as a basis, a skills analysis was prepared emphasising particularly:

- The use of relevant sensory channels;

- The organisation of information;

- Coordination of movement;

- Eye movements.

The type of detailed breakdown is shown in Figure 6.2. Left-hand and right-hand operations are shown together with an indication of which senses are receiving information and governing action with particular reference to kinaesthetic and tactual senses. For this stage, the instructor studied a skilled operator and performed the job himself.

ANALYSIS OF TEACHABLE ELEMENTS

The job was divided into teachable parts based on the trainer's assessment of the learning requirements. Parts were not too large for the operator to absorb and not too small to disrupt the development of rhythm. Key parts were the main flesh cutting strokes.

ANALYSIS OF TEACHING PRIORITIES

Because of the important of yield, those features of the operation affecting yield were given priority. The key factors were:

- The point of entry of the knife;

- The main flesh cutting strokes.

They were taught extremely carefully stressing the impact of yield. Speed was allowed to develop without pressure.

Other features requiring less skill and having less impact on yield were taught at speed from the start, namely:

- Selecting the fish to be filleted;

- Positioning it on the board;

- Moving it to a new position;

- Trimming strokes;

- Placing fillets in the bin;

- Discarding skeletons to the waste bin.

Thus in the early days of training, the trainee was encouraged to make yield strokes deliberately but to move the fish and to trim fillets at speed. The movement of materials was the easiest to train at speed. There was still some reluctance on the part of trainees who were not used to handling a knife to trim with fast strokes. A feature of the yield strokes was that the more correctly they were made the less trimming was necessary and perfect yield strokes usually meant no trimming at all.

The first stages of the training are shown in Figure 6.3. Demonstration of filleting took seven hours on the first day of training. On the second day, the trainee filleted one kit of fish under close observation and then began target exercises.

Figure 6.2 Skills analysis of fish filleting

Dept.: _____

Operation _____   Date: _____

SECTION OR ELEMENT	LEFT HAND	RIGHT HAND	VISION	OTHER SENSES	COMMENTS
Select fish.	Reach to trough grasp fish with T and 1234 around belly. P/U and bring forward to board.	P/U knife with T and 1234 around handle. With sharp edge of blade to the right of filleter.	Glances ahead for knife position on board. Glances ahead for fish position on trough.	Touch – LH on fish.	
Position fish.	Place fish on board so that the dorsal fins fall to the edge of the board and the head lies to the right hand side of the filleter.	Knife Hold: Hold knife handle against the first and third joints of the fingers. Place upper part of T (1st joint) against the lower blunt edge of the knife and the lower part of T against the upper edge of handle Do not grasp knife tightly. Do not curl tip of fingers into palm of hand. Press T against handle for cut.	Checks position of fish.	Touch – LH on fish. LH. Pressure – T on knife.	Knife is held in the RH during the complete filleting cycle. If knife is held correctly it should be possible to move the knife to the left and right by 'opening' and 'closing' the knuckles (when T is removed from handle).
Initial nape cut, remove dorsal portion of pectoral girdle from dorsal muscle.	P/u Pectoral fin with T and 1 and hold at angle of 45° to dorsal muscle (body of fish).	Insert knife under fin and against lug bone. Draw knife down and away to the right – against the skull bone – to the centre back of the head. Raise W when the centre knife blade passes the centre back of head. Finish cut by drawing off the tip of knife.	Observes area between base of fin and dorsal muscle to determine the position of the knife. Glances ahead of the knife – to the centre back of the head.	Touch LH on Pectoral fin. Kinaesthetic – RH feels lug bone against knife. Kinaesthetic – LH feels the skull bone under the knife – This 'guides' the cut.	Use whole blade of knife to cut.

Notes: LH = left hand, RH = right hand, P/U = pick up, T = thumb, 1 = first finger, 2 = second finger, 3 = third finger, 4 = fourth finger, W = wrist. Synchronous movements are recorded in the same line, Successive movements are recorded on succeeding lines.

Figure 6.3   First stages of training programme for fish filleters

ELEMENT	STAGES
Introduction to Department	Trainee is shown the reception, weighing, filleting departments before training begins introduction to department.
1 Job cycle observation	Trainee observes method instructor filleting. Instructor explains the job in general as he is filleting.
2 Identification of fish parts	Instructor points out key parts of fish and asks trainee to name them.
3 Fish handling	Instructor demonstrates how to pick the fish up. Trainee transfers fish one by one.
4 Knife holding	Instructor demonstrates how to hold the knife and how to turn the knife in the hand so that the blade makes one complete circle. Trainee holds and turns blade five times.
5 Fish handling and knife holding exercise	Instructor demonstrates the following: 1 Picks fish up with LH and knife up with RH simultaneously. 2 Places fish on board in first position and turns knife so that sharp edge is to the left of trainee – simultaneously. 3 Picks up fish from board and places it aside – turns knife back to first position. Trainee practices the above exercise until all fish have been transferred.
6 Knife sharpening	Practise knife sharpening.
7 Initial cut	Instructor demonstrates initial cut emphasising: 1 Point of knife insertion. 2 Feel of bone under knife. 3 Direction of cut. 4 LH hold on fish. Trainee makes initial cut on all fish – Transferring them when cut.

ANALYSIS OF LEARNING CURVES

Learning curves were drawn for each operator and after sufficient operators had been trained it was possible to establish norms and cut-off points.

This provided the basis for analysis of the learning process and for later adjustment of training programmes. Three out of four trainees in each group achieved the standard of experienced workers in four weeks at this stage compared with a previous expectation of eight weeks.

Yield figures during training had also improved and there was every reason to be satisfied with the result. However, more information was now available and further analysis and adjustments to the training pattern led to further progress at the next stage.

Development of the Analysis: Stage 2

Analysis at the second stage consisted of a re-examination of the basic facts and a thorough review of the first training experience.

Figure 6.4   Normal learning curve

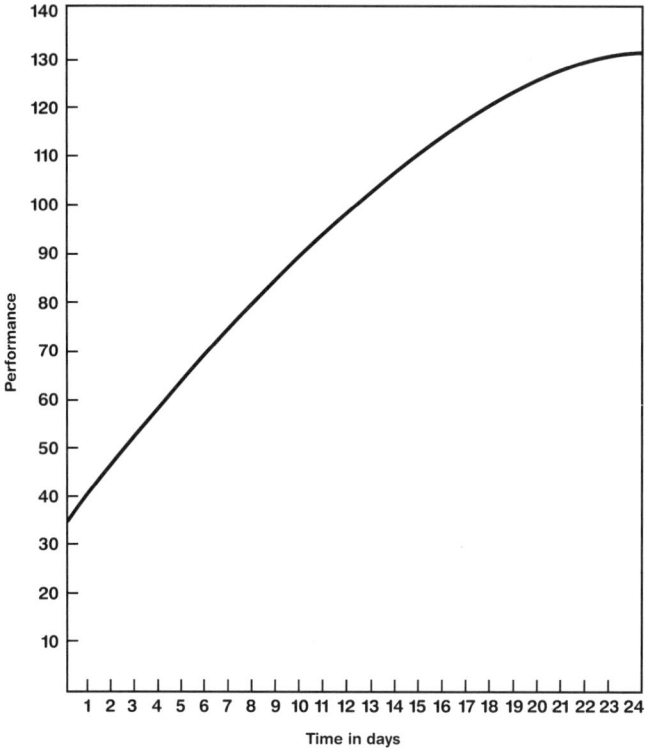

Observations Made Once a Day

ANALYSIS OF SKILL

Although no fundamental changes were made in the skills analysis, some improvements were achieved by experiment and by the use of film. Filming provided a completely new view of the operation and led to the recognition of new aspects of the basic skill, particularly in the cutting strokes. Its success on this particular job accelerated its acceptance and use in a wide range of other areas contributing significantly to the growing impact of training as a whole.

ANALYSIS OF LEARNING CURVES

The normal learning curve, making all allowances for variation in material, is shown in Figure 6.4. This was drawn from observations taken daily and looked quite acceptable. However, when observations were made more frequently in the first four days the curve was more disturbing, as shown in Figure 6.5. Intensification of instruction in the light of this re-examination led to the disappearance of the traditional 'dip' at the second stage.

Observation of those who did not reach the standard of experienced workers (133 on the performance scale) in four weeks showed the major cause was blisters or rashes. The need for some advice on hardening hands before training was started was recognised and acted on.

Figure 6.5   Detailed learning curve

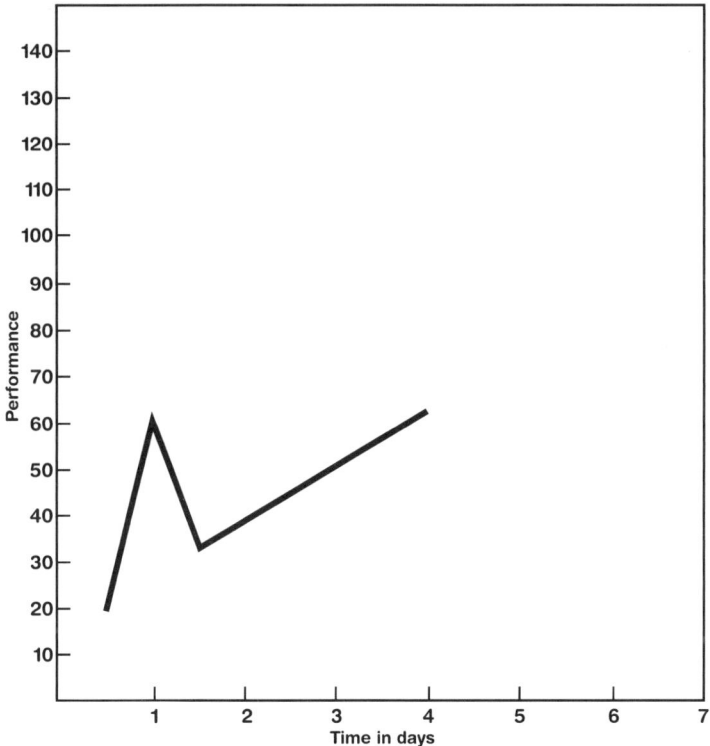

Development of the Analysis: Stage 3

Although the whole operation had been comparatively very successful and encouraging, there were still particular difficulties, namely:

- Production pressure often gave little chance for an instructor to use film or experiment with his analysis.

- As a result, some analysis which could have come earlier was carried out after training was started.

- The output of groups of trainees was difficult to forecast.

- Full control of the training programme came only after a number of operators had been trained.

At this stage the accent had always been on the time taken to learn rather than the amount of work done or the number of attempts before consistent performance was achieved. An MTM research paper[2] describing experiments showing the relationship between learning time and complexity measured by the number of cue motions led to thinking of the possibility of using MTM breakdown analysis for training purposes.

Instructors who have been trained in skills analysis and who work on the system of training as outlined often have no difficulty in visualising a task once it is written down on an MTM breakdown sheet but do require additional information to convert this into a teaching document.

Using MTM analysis as the base material, the difficulties recognised can be overcome by the following additions to the analysis:

1.   Analysis of skill:

   a. Symbols for specific sensory channels are added using the cases of movement as an indication that the work is being carried out without consistent visual control.

   b. Cue motion values are added for each movement.

---

2   Methods-Time Measurement Research Studies Report 114 – *Factors in Manual Skill Training (MTM Association).*

2. Analysis of teachable elements. Teachable elements are defined on the basis of a maximum of 12 cue motion associations forming an ideal element instead of on the basis of the subjective assessment of the trainer.

3. Analysis of teaching priorities. Distances shown on the MTM breakdown sheet are used to indicate speed training priorities.

4. Analysis of learning curves:

    a) The number of attempts to achieve performance is established on the basis of complexity measured by the number of cue motions.

    b) This is converted to standard hours to provide a meaningful target for training.

    c) A mean learning curve is applied to this for the task concerned bearing in mind the department and method of payment which will effect motivation of the learner.

Figure 6.6   MTM cut-off line

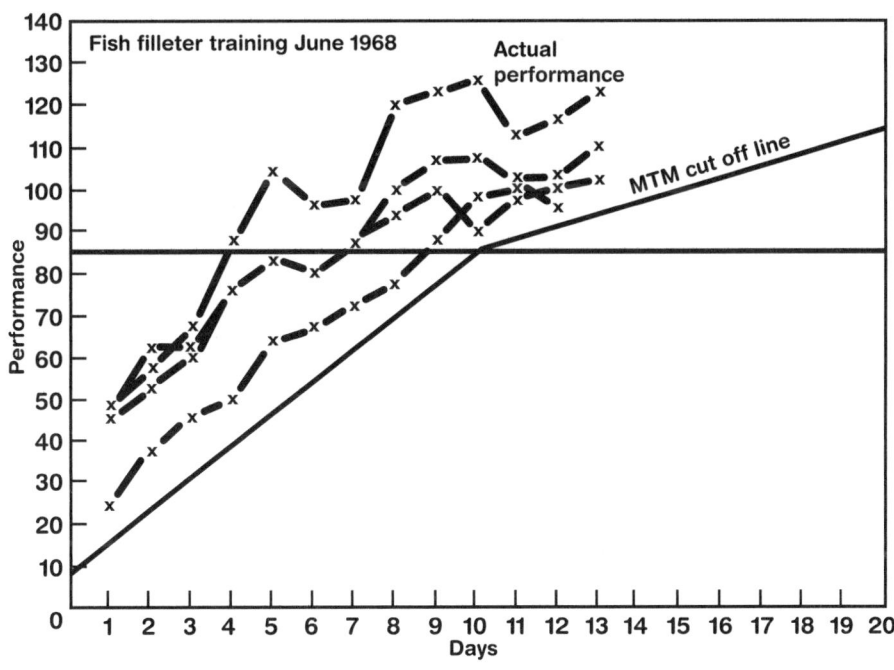

d)   The length of the training period is determined and a cut-off line plotted. This is illustrated in Figure 6.6.

Links with Broader Training Problems

Although this case example is a very special illustration of analysis at operator level, it was also very valuable as an introduction to the analysis of other training problems. The links with other problems developed particularly in two ways; line information and the use of film.

LINE INFORMATION

The work of the instructors in carrying out detailed skills analysis provided a pattern which was seen to be of clear value in other production areas and on other types of operations. Initially it provided the basis of training manuals mainly for operator training but it was not long before this information was seen to be crucial for manager and supervisors as well.

FILM ANALYSIS

The use of film analysis enables training problems to be reviewed at group basis. Although the focus was initially on the problems of operatives, the group discussion provided a means of widening the objectives and for looking at the total learning situation.

On-line training reviewed in Chapter 16 provides similar and added opportunities.

7

Case Study 2: Operation of a Special Purpose Machine and Learning Design

This case study is concerned with the analysis and training preparation associated with the introduction of a special purpose packaging machine. Details of the machine will only be included if they are relevant to the analysis. The training thinking associated with the machine and its environment and the relevance of the problem to broad training policy will be emphasised.

This case study provides a good illustration of problem recognition and analysis at a number of levels. It emphasises the distinction between job analysis and training needs analysis. Although it is concerned with a specialist operation, wide general lessons can be derived from it. Links with the broad development of training are illustrated in terms of:

- the trainer's approach to problems at various levels in an organisation;

- the steady establishment of a basic validity and credibility for training.

Background

The organisation is the same as that in the first case study. Here the problem is adjustment to rapid and costly technology innovation. The machine was one of several introduced to deal with a range of special packaging problems. The introduction of similar machines had been accompanied by many problems and unsatisfactory performance.

Opinions at various levels suggested major learning and training problems. Losses from machine breakdown and stoppage, mainly in the run-in period, had been estimated as being over £200,000 per annum in man-hours alone. On the basis of the 'plan for training needs analysis' (Chapter 5) the first analysis showed:

- First impression: score 4 to 5

  Considerable skill and knowledge problems, evidence of other learning problems, probably good pay-off, problems hardly understood, managers involved in the learning process.

- Associated problems: score 4 to 5

  Some links with other jobs which frustrate the learning in the area, broader organisational problems probably a major consideration.

- The trainee view, score 5

  Extensive problems little understood.

- Trainer view, score 4 to 5

  Extensive skill and knowledge problems only partially understood.

- The operational view: score 4

  Complex job partially understood, vague objectives and limited controls.

The high overall score left little doubt of the high priority for training. In this case the need for training was also clearly recognised by the manufacturer of the machine.

The situation is in many ways a classic training challenge. From the trainer's point of view it provides a first-class entry point into a whole range of engineering training problems. From the operational point of view success is likely to bring great rewards and will provide every incentive for changes in skill, attitude and organisation.

Initial Detailed Analysis

Initial work concentrated on a thorough analysis of the machine in use. There were two major assumptions:

- That the major learning problem was to provide craftsmen with knowledge of the machine.

- The main requirement was therefore an early and systematic analysis of the structure and operation of the machine. This implied a good and comprehensive machine manual which could be used for reference and as the basis for specific training. Extracts from a training manual are given in Appendix 7a.

Although these two factors remained salient features of the training development, it soon became clear that the early assumptions needed considerable modification. In particular it was recognised that:

- Although the knowledge content of the associated work was great, the activity (skill) content should not be underestimated.

- A large proportion of the mental activity involved was diagnostic – recognising and tracing faults. In addition to knowledge of the plant this requires:

  a. detailed observation;

  b. recognition of symptoms;

  c. 'Eliminatory' thinking, that is thinking which leads to the elimination of non-operative causes of faults and the determination of the true cause. Finding the quickest way to communicate this important skill, which may not be directly related to general engineering knowledge is a major training problem. The original training manual required considerable modification to meet the training needs.

- Many learning problems existed at other levels.

As anticipated in the first assessment, training needs existed at a number of levels. These became clearer as the work progressed.

Craft Training Need

The basic craft need was clear from the start and the need for diagnostic skill gave another dimension to the problem. Although of major importance, the craft elements did not present the greatest difficulties of recognition of need.

Operator Training Need

Basic operator needs did not emerge as early as they might have done. In retrospect, a more thorough analysis of the available data may have clarified the situation sooner, but the early stages of training are always likely to give further insight into certain needs. In fact the training should always be geared to allow for this.

During the early stages of the analysis it became clear that operators had a vital role to play in eliminating faults at the feed stage. Training was therefore focused on recognising key cues, principally the slight distortions in pack or product essential for the machine to operate to the very fine adjustment necessary for maximum through-put.

Supervisory and Management Training Need

At this level the basic knowledge requirements were soon generally recognised. Engineering supervisors in particular needed to be aware of the basic data in the main machine manual. The major problem was a much broader management training difficulty. Concepts of training possibilities were very limited. Production managers recognised the basic operational needs. Engineers were generally sceptical and saw only a relatively limited need for providing information. The wider possibilities of the much more streamlined learning process envisaged in the overall training programme were not recognised. They had to be learnt. This was achieved by personal persuasion backed by the results from the training programme as it progressed.

Organisational Development Need

The progress of the training made it possible to look much more deeply into related organisational problems. It triggered a complete review of the training role in the engineering area and the problems of communication and information flow related to packaging machinery in particular. As a result, the need for organisational changes and relearning were recognised. A much more effective 'early warning system' was built into the organisation, providing for the more extensive introduction of new machinery which was planned. Line management recognised much more clearly the training role in this introductory process and in other ways. The trainer's role was accepted and redefined in the production area and the technical development areas as illustrated in the job descriptions given as an Appendix to Chapter 1.

Lessons

This study illustrates the evolutionary nature of training analysis. The trainers involved started by dealing with a recognised knowledge problem at a relatively simple level. At each stage, however, the training was designed to allow for further and more sophisticated diagnosis. As the diagnosis was extended, the trainers stimulated rethinking and were able to contribute to problems of increasing complexity at higher levels. The move was from instructor, to management trainer, to change agent. It demonstrated that internal trainers can move quickly towards the analysis of essential, high-level problems, by starting from the root rather than the top.

In addition to this, more specific lessons were learnt about the detailed analysis required of machine knowledge. At the start of the project the manuals emerging differed very little from the standard manufacturers' manual: emphasis was on what the machine did. It was soon recognised that from a training point of view material had to be completely recategorised. Emphasis had to be put on what needed to be learnt. The information was arranged in such a way that it provided a basic syllabus for each item and was geared to particular levels of trainee.

It was found that normal training processes could not deal with the complexities of fault analysis. The parts of the training dealing with faults were gradually condensed. The question of teaching the diagnostic skill involved in fault-finding led to much more thorough experiments in establishing courses for this particular purpose. An example is the training produced for apprentices and fitters which is described in Appendix 7b.

Appendix 7a: Training Manual for a Packaging Machine

The analysis described in Chapter 7 showed that a comprehensive manual was necessary for training operators of the packaging machinery. Excerpts from a manual are given in this Appendix. The training programme, which is summarised in Figure 7.1, is intensive and relies heavily on repetition. Stages 2, 3, 4, 7, 11, 15 and 16 each consist of a period of instruction followed by a complete recapitulation by the trainee. In stages 8 and 9 the trainee also performs the tasks that have just been taught. In the three revision periods, stages 5, 10 and 17, both instructor and trainee repeat the information given before.

Only 75 minutes of the training period are spent in a training room. The remainder is spent in the production area applying knowledge.

For section *B* of the training, the manual gives a description of the important elements in each area of the machine. The section on the heat-sealing and photo-electric cell (PEC) areas is given in Figure 7.2.

On the second day of training, the instructor again goes over the identification of each part of each area of the machine and adds in the possible faults. The manual contains details of possible faults and the necessary action: the section on the wrapping material and PEC areas is given in Figure 7.3. The instructor must not rely on memory in this stage of the training but must use the manual. When the instructor has explained the possible faults in each area, the trainees explain them again in their own words.

TRAINING OBJECTIVES

What the trainee is expected to do and know when the training programme is completed:

- must be able to identify the parts of the machine correctly;

- must be familiar with the 'troublesome' areas of the machine;

- must be able to start and stop the machine correctly;

- must be able to thread the machine in 15 seconds;

- must be able to feed the machine quickly, while watching the finished product leave the machine;

- must be able to check the running machine for possible faults;

- must be able to explain to a fitter the cause of a breakdown and know when to call the fitter to correct minor faults in order to prevent a major breakdown;

- must know how to complete the faults records.

It is the responsibility of the method instructor to ensure that the trainee can meet the above objectives at the end of training.

Figure 7.1   Training programme for packaging machinery operation

SECTION	NO.	STAGE	APPROX TIME IN MINUTES
A	1	*Introduction to the department* Visit department – show trainee work performed with special emphasis on the machine. Allow trainee to stand and watch the experienced worker on the machine.	30
B		*Training room or room off the production area* Learning and identification of machine details and adjustments in the following order	
	2	*Volumetric area* The identification of the volumetric parts of the machine – on photograph The correct name of each part; its purpose (use) and any adjustments made on that part	15
	3	*Wrapping material feed area* The identification of the wrapping material feed parts of the machine The correct name of each part; its purpose (use) and any adjustments made on that part	15
	4	*Heat sealing and PEC area* The identification of the heat-sealing and PEC (photo-electric cell) parts of the machine The correct name for each part; its purpose (use) and any adjustments made on that part	15
		BREAK: 15 minutes	
C	5	*Revision of stages 2–4*	30
	6	*Observation on factory floor* The machine parts and purpose are identified by trainee on the machine and checked by instructor The trainee observes an experienced worker on the machine for the remainder of the 60 minutes	1 hr 45 mins

Figure 7.1   Continued

SECTION	NO.	STAGE	APPROX TIME IN MINUTES
D	7	*Control panel* The identification of the control panel switch knobs and rotary breaks The correct name of the knob; its purpose and who to use it	60
	8	*Starting procedure* The rules for starting the machine at the beginning of shift – demonstrated by instructor The rules for starting the machine after a brief shut-down period – demonstrated by instructor	10
	9	*Stopping procedure* The rules for stopping the machine at the end of shift – demonstrated by instructor The rules for stopping the machine during the shift – demonstrated by instructor	20
E	10	*Revision of stages 7–9*	20
	11	*Running procedure checklist* Instructor points out to trainee the key points which require attention during the running of the machine – instructor uses the manual	25
	12	*Observation on machine* The trainee identifies the control panel and explains the starting and stopping procedures Trainee makes a running check on the machine Trainee identifies all the parts and purpose of the machine. Instructor checks carefully to ensure that the above stages are understood by trainee	30
F	13	*Remainder of shift* Trainee starts, stops and checks the machine and bags for the remainder of the shift Trainee also makes any necessary adjustments to machine Instructor demonstrates the reel preparation and reel change – and trainee prepares and changes the reels for the remainder of shift	60 To End of Shift 8 Hours
G	14	SECOND DAY *Fault procedure: factory floor* *Volumetric area* Instructor asks trainee to identify the parts, use, and any adjustments made on the volumetric area of the machine (as for Stage 2) Instructor explains: the fault that arises in each part; the reason for the fault (cause); what action to take if fault occurs (remedial action); and how to prevent that fault from occurring (prevention)	

Figure 7.1   Continued

SECTION	NO.	STAGE	APPROX TIME IN MINUTES
H	15	*Wrapping material feed area* Instructor asks trainee to identify the parts, use and any adjustments made on the wrapping material feed area (Stage 3) Instructor explains: the fault that arises in each part; the reason for the fault (causes); what action to take if fault occurs (remedial action); and how to prevent that fault from occurring (prevention)	30
	16	*Heat-sealing and PEC area* Instructor asks trainee to identify the parts, use and any adjustments made in the heat-sealing area (Stage 4) Instructor explains: the fault that arises in each part; the reason for the fault (cause); what action to be taken if fault occurs (remedial action); and how to prevent that fault from occurring (prevention)	30
	17	*Revision of stages 14, 15 and 16*	
I	18	*Reel change/preparation/threading* (a) Instructor checks that trainee prepares the reel correctly, and changes it correctly and quickly (15 seconds) (b) Instructor allows reel on machine to run out and demonstrates reel threading (c) Trainee attempts to remove and replace forming shoulder and spreader until they can do so correctly and within one minute	30
J	19	*Cleaning procedure* Instructor explains the importance of cleanliness to trainee – demonstrates cleaning the machine, with emphasis on the sealing bars and machine parts	15
	20	*Safety* The instructor explains the reason for the guard doors and the danger of grasping the bag while it is being sealed	5

Figure 7.2   Machine details and adjustments, heat-sealing and PEC area

DETAIL	USE	ADJUSTMENT
Longitudinal seal bar	Seals back seal of bag	–
Longitudinal seal heater on control panel	For fine and coarse temperature adjustment	For slight increase in temperature graduate to higher *stroke*
Longitudinal seal switch on control panel	Heats sealing wire	For course increase – graduate to higher *number*
Teflon	Sealing material over the sealing wires of both longitudinal and cross seals	If dirty – clean with plastic If worn/torn/burnt } call fitter for replacement
Grippers	Material for gripping bag when Cross sealed	Check that grippers are positioned *above* and *below* sealing wire If dirty – clean with plastic scraper
Cross seal bars	Seals top and bottom edges of bags	–
End seal volts switch on control panel	For fine and coarse adjustment of temperature	For *fine* increase in temperature graduate to higher *stroke* For *coarse* increase in temperature graduate to higher *number*
PEC scanning head	PEC – photo-electric cell This projects a beam onto wrapping material, the beam alters when scanning the register mark on paper. This reflection is amplified by the amplifier (inside machine) which causes the cross seal bars to open – thus ensuring that the same bag length is cut off every time	PEC should scan register mark on paper. If NOT: Unscrew locking screw (9) by turning to the left. Turn adjusting knob (10) to the right to move unit up track (11) and turn knob (10) to left to bring unit down track. When PEC is in correct position turn locking screw (9) to right to secure

Figure 7.3   Possible faults: PEC wrapping material area

APPEARANCE OF FAULTS	POSSIBLE CAUSES	REMEDIAL ACTION	PREVENTION	POINTS TO NOTE AND SIDE EFFECTS
Wet or partly wet paper – paper clinging to tube 'Sticky' paper.	1 Reel placed on wet surface. 2 Incorrect storage.	1 Remove reel immediately. 2 Rethread machine with dry reel.	1 Inspect reel before placing on machine.	
Shoulder jam (torn paper under collar of forming shoulder).	1 Clumsy joining of reels – paper caught under collar. 2 Paper wet under collar.	1 Remove spreader and forming shoulder. Push sealing tube back-up adjustment to side. Wrap paper around tube. Replace shoulder spreader and back up. 2 Dry tube before replacing paper.	1 Make neat-reel joinings. 2 Check tip of forming tube for condensation before starting machine.	If this fault has occurred – check that the cross seals, knife and groove are free from the waste product which has fallen on the machine seals after paper tear and before stopping machine.
Picture positioned incorrectly on bag, e.g., too high/low.	1 Length variation from old to new seal. 2 PEC out of alignment.	1 Adjust PEC vertically by unscrewing locking screw and turning the adjusting knob down if picture is too high on bag and vice versa.	1 Join old to new reel so that no extra paper will be added to first bag.	Do not adjust PEC unless absolutely necessary.

Appendix 7b: Systematic Approach to Trouble-Shooting on Packaging Machinery

Although they are given basic information, the majority of trouble-shooters do not diagnose faults in the best possible way. Much of their knowledge is acquired by trial and error. In some cases faults are corrected by chance; the reason for the fault or the actual adjustment made is unknown, since multiple adjustments are made without testing each one. No learning results from this unsystematic approach.

Systematic approaches to fault-finding have been extensively examined. More details will be found in Dale's book listed in the Bibliography. Figure 7.4 summarises the steps that must be followed when systematically diagnosing faults.

TRAINING COURSE

The experimental course described in this Appendix had three aims:

- to introduce apprentices and fitters to two packaging machines;

- to provide the trainees with a clear, concise method of trouble-shooting by presenting them with a number of rules to follow;

- to train them to write fault diagnosis for the machines.

MACHINES

First, a 'closer' machine was chosen because:

- it could be transported easily into the training room – away from the shop floor, and hence provide a more favourable learning situation;

- the machine was relatively simple in comparison with other machinery in production and this safeguarded any danger of being over-engrossed in the machine and unreceptive to the system;

- a large number of faults could be simulated on the machine and this provided an excellent opportunity to test the knowledge of the trainees and to use the actual machine in teaching instead of visual aids.

Figure 7.4   Systematic approach to trouble-shooting

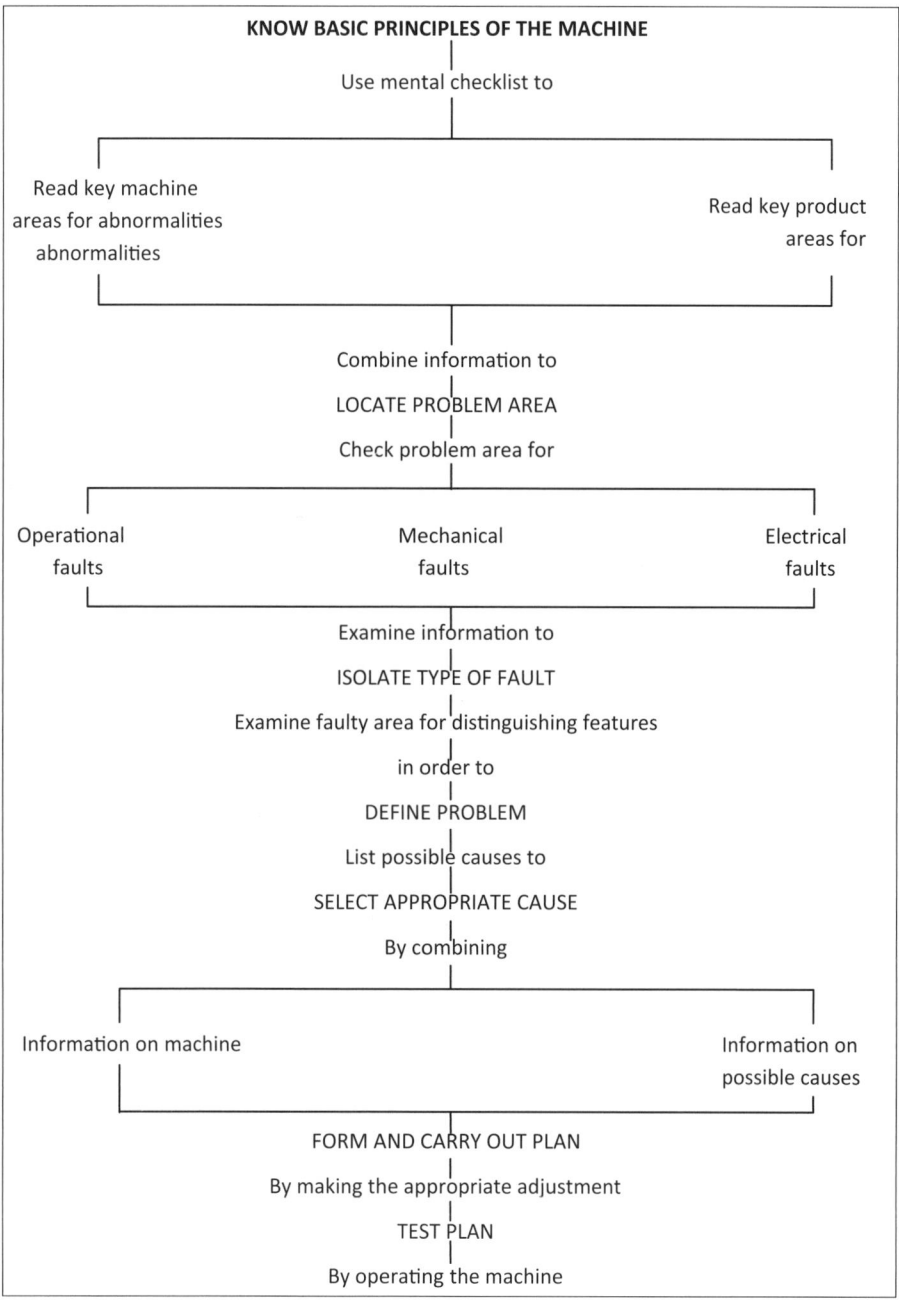

As knowledge of the machine improves, the system is reduced to the seven stages set in capital letters and intermediate stages are bypassed.

The other machine was used because:

- it is possibly the most common packaging machine on site;

- it is also a complex machine and it was necessary to know how well the system worked with complex machinery as with simple machinery.

PROGRAMME

The course lasted for three days and ran from 09:00 to 16:00 with 30-minute lunch break and two 15-minute tea breaks.

The course began with general information and gradually became more specific and detailed. An appreciation talk was given on general packaging machinery and packaging materials followed by a general introduction to the 'closer' machine. This was then divided into three main areas, with a detailed description of each area, its purpose and settings. For demonstration purposes the machine was set correctly at this stage.

RESULTS

The course was run four times, first with apprentices and then with fitters. With the apprentices a reduction of 17 minutes was achieved in the average time taken to diagnose faults. The course was also successful with experienced fitters. The main problem was that trainees found it difficult to combine the information about procedure with information provided by the machine and the product. They found difficulty in remembering which stage of the systematic approach they were on. This was overcome by insisting on oral repetition of the stages of the system until it was 'learned' and semi-automatic.

Appendix 7c: Broader Contributions to Learning Design

The following diagrams summarise key aspects of training and learning design at all levels. The training cycle provides a useful introduction to reviewing training at all levels in an organisation. The Group Feedback Analysis is a useful preliminary tool for any group which is about to embark on training of any kind.

Figure 7.5   Learning design

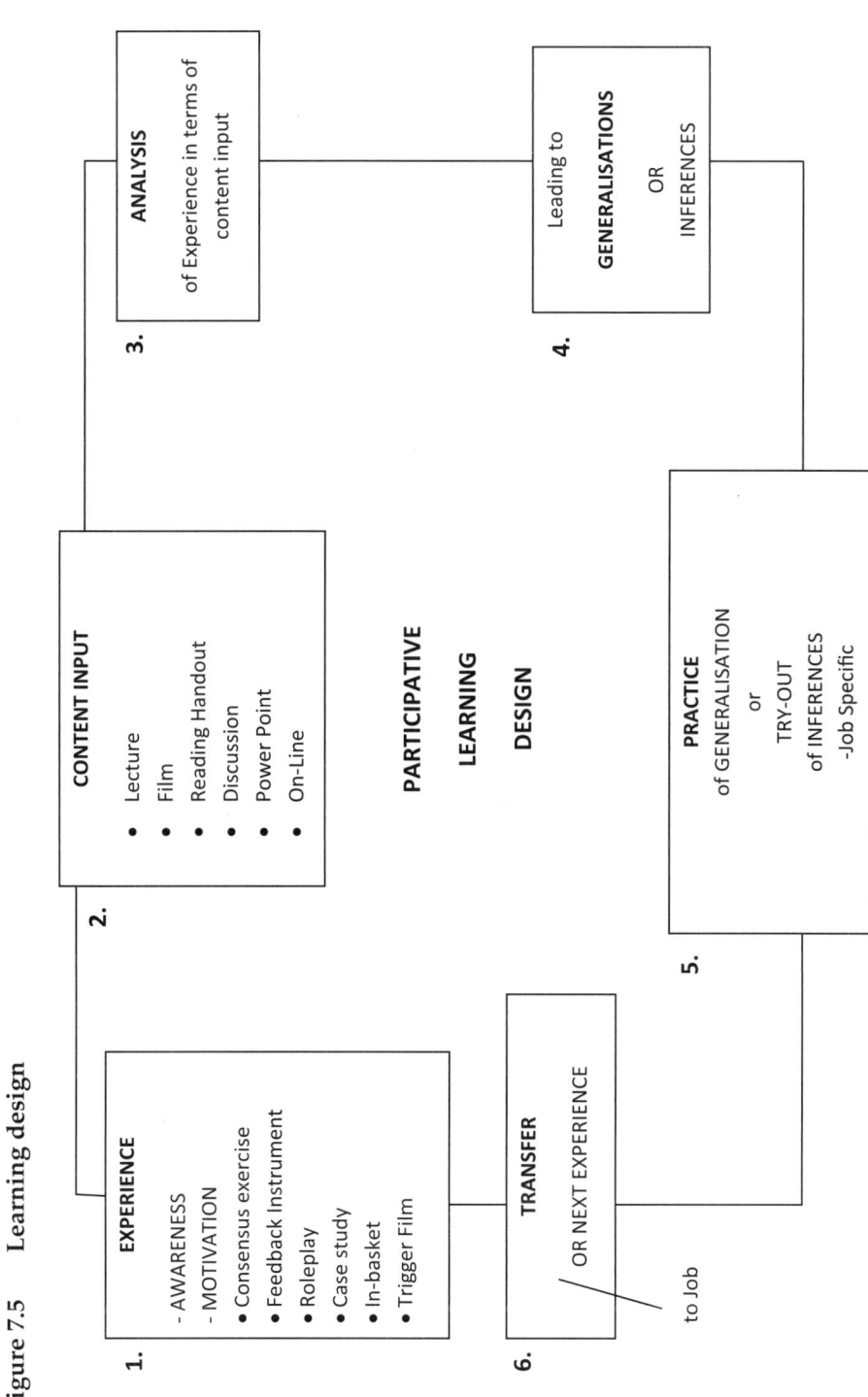

Figure 7.6   The training cycle

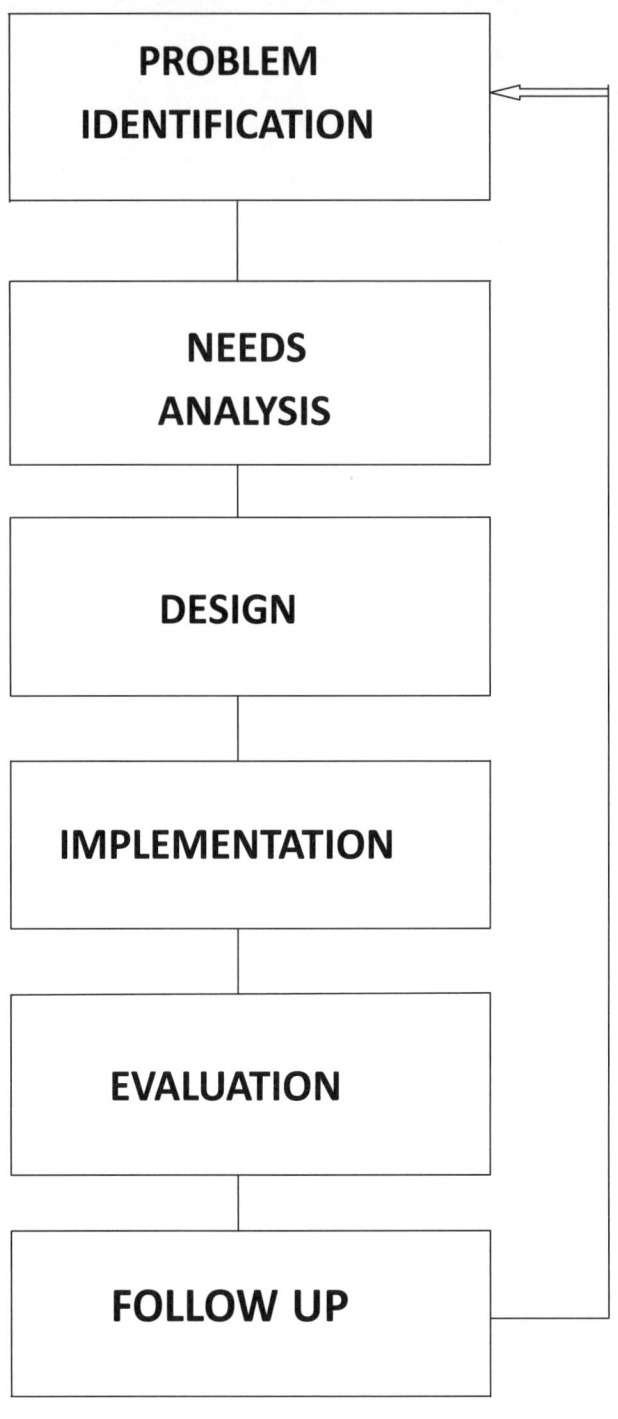

Figure 7.7   Learning at work

Please assess the extent to which you agree or disagree with each of the following statements and circle the appropriate number.

0 = strongly disagree
6 = strongly agree

1   Experience is the best teacher

         0   1   2   3   4   5   6

2   'If the learner hasn't learned, the teacher hasn't taught'

         0   1   2   3   4   5   6

3   The only measure of training is a change in behaviour

         0   1   2   3   4   5   6

4   Most courses are a waste of time and money

         0   1   2   3   4   5   6

5   People learn best with and from each other

         0   1   2   3   4   5   6

6   People don't learn much from ISO 9000

         0   1   2   3   4   5   6

7   Learning means change

         0   1   2   3   4   5   6

8   I know what I need to learn

         0   1   2   3   4   5   6

9   My organisation offers good training

         0   1   2   3   4   5   6

10   Organisations that don't learn don't survive

         0   1   2   3   4   5   6

8

Management Training Analysis

Ideas about management training have developed in a number of quite distinct ways. This has affected the approach to analysis of management training needs. Various schools of thought have had their own emphasis. The main approaches have been:

- An educational process, particularly concerned with the links between business schools and industry.

- A management development approach, primarily concerned with planning and training for those few managers with exceptionally high potential.

- The job training approach, concerned with raising the standards of all managers in skills relevant to their particular jobs.

All three of these approaches can be seen at the present time, although they are now tending to merge in a broader operational approach. However, their existence has affected thinking about training analysis and, therefore, this chapter will be divided into three main parts covering the main schools of thought.

Management Education

It is at the management level that the distinction between the relative merits of the educational and the operation-based approach are most clearly indicated. Because of the difficulty of establishing a top-level starting point for internal training, most management training has, in fact, developed away from the job and frequently away from industry. One of the biggest growth areas in education has been that concerned with management studies in the colleges and universities. Many companies have established their own 'colleges' in suitable halls and stately homes where the atmosphere is usually academic as opposed to industrial. The syllabuses of management courses in company training centres frequently differ little from those provided by colleges except that economic pressure often ensures that courses are more condensed.

Although this separatist attitude has obvious limitations, it is not without advantages. It has led to the creation of departments of business studies in universities and independent foundations that form a spearhead of new thinking, particularly about the techniques of management. It has, however, not always helped the development of concepts of internal industry-based management training focused on the improvement of management and organisation performance and on the practice of management.

Initial analysis of training needs at management level, often encouraged to a large extent by the common management view that training is something organised by an outside educator, have largely been attempts to fill particular knowledge gaps. The thinking involved is of three kinds which can be called 'the broadening approach,' 'the management education approach,' and 'the techniques approach'.

BROADENING APPROACH

The assumption here is that management education is of general value in raising personal and social standards and that this will benefit industry in the long run by giving a broader outlook, ensuring that management decisions are taken within the context of a full appreciation of the environmental factors involved. The basic view that managers are born and not made still lingers, but there is recognition that even the 'natural' manager must have a very full appreciation of the facts about the world one lives in.

Analysis

The analysis associated with this approach leads to the recognition of the need for influential middle managers and those with high potential to attend general management background courses. This is also usually linked with the view that self-development is of the utmost importance and that every opportunity should be provided for managers who wish to study in their own time to do so. Continuing professional development is encouraged and reinforced by professional bodies.

Training programme

This will involve provision for evening and part-time study for business qualifications as well as short general management courses concerned with management principles and human relations. Senior management would normally be encouraged to attend 'conferences' which enable them to keep in touch with new thinking associated with the management field.

MANAGEMENT EDUCATION APPROACH

Management education is recognised as making at least an indirect contribution to profits in the long term. It is seen as being of considerable help in keeping the company up to date and in touch with other companies' activities. It is seen as being particularly vital for managers who are moving quickly through the company and are likely to be in senior positions in a few years time.

Analysis

The analysis makes it clear that management training is certainly necessary in the long term and should be provided and encouraged as long as it does not interfere with short-term priorities. There is an indication that priority should be given to the training of managers in a 'management development scheme'. Much of the learning is expected to take place by the exchange of ideas between participants.

Training programme

Private study and business study courses involving some day release are involved as well as special short courses for middle managers allowing particularly for 'cross fertilisation'. Top-level courses at universities and independent colleges are provided for 'high flyers'.

TECHNIQUES APPROACH

It is clearly recognised that management training pays off in the long term. A techniques revolution is recognised and it is widely thought to be essential to fill the gaps in knowledge bound to occur in this situation as quickly as possible. In some areas a short-term impact is recognised as, for instance, in the harnessing of computer knowledge and skills.

Analysis

With this approach the analysis begins to go much deeper than previously and to look for individual knowledge gaps as opposed to the general requirement of a body of managers. Analysis becomes more thorough. Questions concerned with training, particularly specific shortcomings in terms of knowledge and skill, are incorporated in appraisal systems. Knowledge and skill requirements are categorised.

Training programme

Internal and external techniques courses are sought at all levels. Wide use is made of general management courses with a teaching and techniques bias. Internally, new techniques are explored which are likely to make a rapid contribution to fill in the gaps of knowledge and skill which have been recognised. Programmed learning material and e-learning is likely to be introduced on a wide scale.

Most management training systems today will involve some elements of all these approaches and provided that they are in the right perspective they will be entirely sound. On the whole, however, they do represent an early stage in the development of thinking and the important facet to consider at this point is the relationship of the programmes to the background thinking and analysis. Partial analysis can only produce a partially relevant training programme. At all stages it is impossible to emphasise too strongly the need to probe continuously for the real learning problems and training needs, recognising that these needs will stem from the operational requirements and the whole management structure involving a team as well as individuals. The shortcomings of this approach are that the management group is either seen as an amorphous mass with rather vague general training needs, or where an individual analysis is made it is in fact only concerned with certain aspects of knowledge and skill.

The analysis behind this type of management education must inevitably be very general. Essentially it was related to what has become known as the 'common skills' approach, although it could be more fairly described as the 'common knowledge' approach. Much recent work has tended to question the basic validity of this approach. Stress has been rightly laid on the need for detailed job analysis and this has been seen essentially as a move away from common skills. This is not necessarily so unless the job analysis relates to a very limited operational area. If the analysis does cover a wide organisational area, common skills as well as particular skills are bound to emerge. Dangers in the past have been:

- that the analysis has been superficial as well as general, syllabuses were concerned with a very broad view of what industry was thought likely to require;

- links between common background training and operational activity have not been properly developed;

- the emphasis is on knowledge rather than skill, making links with practical situations more difficult to develop.

In spite of the difficulties and the frequently superficial and detached nature of the analysis, management education related to these approaches is now extremely well developed in a number of areas. Trainers in most areas of the country should have little difficulty in finding very high standard courses. The important thing is to recognise that most of the activities will have been established following a very wide and general analysis of training needs. The trainer must, therefore, be very selective in using the facilities provided to ensure that as far as possible courses line up with the detailed and specific analysis of good local and operational requirements.

At times when hard-nosed financial survival is the priority, there is a danger that much training and some standards, such as Investors in People, are seen as soft and idealistic. ISO 9000, perhaps provides a better basis for a more hard-nosed approach to management improvement based as it is on the following key principles.

Customer Focus

Without customer value, shareholder value can be deceptive, distortive and short lived. There are many ways of keeping track of customer reactions. Surveys, point of sale reactions and market analysis are all important, but the real need is to understand what customers really want. The subtle, not quite intuitive, perceptions of the sales force are as important as responses to questionnaires.

The evidence of customer focus is found at every point of customer contact from point of sale and point of payment, through every aspect of customer service to the priorities given to customer contacts and needs at top level. New product and service development is as important as identification of current needs. A marketing mentality free from spin and deception is needed.

The Standard says:

> *Organisations depend on their customers and therefore should understand current and future needs should meet customer requirements and strive to exceed customer expectations.*

Leadership

Leadership is seen and felt. It is recognised by the clarity and sharpness of the organisational picture. Vagueness, confusion and contradictions are the evidence of failure. Internal conflict and destructive competitiveness are evidence of complete failure. In a team environment, leadership is clearly shared. Responsibility is integrated as well as defined. In the context of the Standard, leadership reflects a coherent set of general standards and values. There is evidence of synthesis as well as analysis.

The Standard says:

> *Leaders establish unity of purpose and direction in an organisation. they should create and maintain the internal environment in which people can become fully involved in achieving an organisation's objectives.*

Involvement of People

The Standard itself is in danger of being vague in this area although there are strict requirements for communication and representation. Nevertheless, autocratic management by decree is clearly out of tune and can be clearly recognised. Positive evidence includes the treatment of people at all levels as thinking, intelligent, adults worthy of respect. Frank and open communication quickly becomes clear in any audit discussion as well as the appreciation and tolerance of humour. Boredom and resentment can be evidence of failure. 'We haven't got time' can be a danger signal.

The Standard says:

> *People at all levels are the essence of an organisation and their full involvement enables their abilities to be used for the organisations benefit.*

Process Approach

The assumption is that management is about recognising and coordinating the key processes of an operation. Most operations will have processes related to:

Finding work

Doing work

Getting paid

Public services will have processes related to:

Defining rules

Doing work

Achieving results

Failures of concern to auditors are frequently related to the links between one process and another, with the danger increasing in proportion to the number of people involved. Another important activity is to check the balance between key processes. A danger is to put a disproportionate amount of effort into one at the expense of another.

The Standard says:

> *A desired result is achieved more efficiently when related resources and activites are managed as a process.*

System Approach to Management

Overall systems of control integrate an organisation. Auditors are trained to spot signs of disintegration even when things appear to be going smoothly. They provide an early warning system. Potential breakdowns are often overlooked because senior managers underestimate the ability of experienced people to compensate for procedural and electronic failures. Intelligent people keep the wheels turning. Major failures often occur when these people are moved to fit into some new organisation pattern which looks good and, maybe, economical on paper.

Changing the 'sticks and boxes' of an organisation without considering the integration and integrity of the new system and possible new links between people and processes can be disastrous.

The Standard says:

> *Identifying, understanding and managing a system of interrelated processes as a system, contributes to an organisation's effectiveness and efficiency in achieving its objectives.*

Continual Improvement

The heavy emphasis in the Standard on measurement, analysis and improvement is reasonable and, in many ways, an auditors dream. Checking numbers, objectives and achievements makes an important contribution to progress, but it is also important to remember that it is possible to measure the wrong things and have too many indicators. Auditors can help by recognising the leading variables – the things that really make a difference, and that subjective as well as objective judgements are allowed. Deming, the Total Quality guru said that 'accounting-based measures of performance drive employers to achieve targets of sales, revenue and costs by manipulation of processes'. People are clever and can deal with complexities better than some systems and measurements can. It is easier to count the bottles than describe the wine. When looking at competence, auditors can help to clarify ideas about perceived quality and as well as basic economics. Quality in a restaurant is about enjoyment and atmosphere as well as profit.

The Standard says:

Continual improvement of an organisation's overall performance should be a permanent objective of the organisation.

Factual Approach to Decision Making

Decision making is an art as well as a science, but the purpose of decision making is to make the best possible choice based on sound information and an assessment of probabilities and possibilities. The revolutionary ideas of modern times relate to the mastery of risk (Bernstein, 1996).

Auditing decision making is first a search for inaccurate and incomplete information. The aim is to improve the quality of information being processed. It is then a process of risk assessment, in particular a rigorous appraisal of the adverse consequences of any decision. The art of decision making is in the generation of a wide range of options in the first place – creativity.

Auditing examines the accuracy of 'facts' the calculations of risk and the generation of ideas. Ideas are facts as well!

The Standard says:

Effective decisions are based on an analysis of data and information.

Mutually Beneficial Supplier Relationships

It is now customary to talk about the 'supply chain'. This is the sequence of processes which leads through product and service realisation to customer satisfaction. There have been many examples of one part of the chain trying to exploit another with disastrous results. Some would say that there are still too many examples of supplier exploitation particularly in the 'third world'. The Standard is clear. It looks for evidence of beneficial relationships. Evidence will be found in top management attitudes and in marketing thinking that goes beyond the four 'P's (product, price, promotion and place) to long-term relationships that produce the economies of cooperation.

The Standard says:

> *An organisation and its suppliers are interdependent and a mutually beneficial relationship enhances the ability of both to create value.*

Management Development

Although the general analysis related to management education can provide a starting point for a trainer seeking to make a more penetrating audit of requirements, it is far from ideal. Management development activities can provide a better foundation because of their closer links with the operational activities of individuals.[1]

If some development work has already been started there are tactical advantages in extending its scope to provide links with wider performance problems. Even in a company without any management training activity it can provide the entry point for a new trainer. If the general need for long-term management and manpower planning is recognised, the mechanism developed for this purpose can be used to provide the basis for a more complete audit of training at this level. This will look at the short-term as well as the long-term improvements in performance.

The first step in this kind of analysis is when top management clearly recognise the need to provide for the long-term development of managers with high potential. This is seen as having a very crucial influence on the growth of the business and of being a key factor in the use of resources.

The analysis will require a regular review of those with high potential. A need for detailed career patterning will be recognised and alongside this specific training gaps will be recognised which will have to be fitted in to the general plan for development.

A systematic review structure will be established. High-level general courses at universities and colleges will be planned ahead of development.

---

1   In this context, the term 'management development' is used to cover all those activities concerned with training and appraisal for promotion or for future, as opposed to present responsibilities, together with the associated activities concerned with placement and planning for succession including Management Standards.

Priority will be given to courses relating to management techniques in line with each stage of development.

Review Structure

The structure designed to meet these management development requirements may take many forms, but key elements will be typical, representing various views about the company and its organisation which will be of immense value to the trainer in working towards a fuller and more operationally-based analysis of the total situation.

THE BOSS'S INDEPENDENT VIEW

This can be obtained formally either as part of a broader appraisal system or by a special questionnaire. The kind of questions which may be related to potential or training requirements are described below. Although it would be dangerous to take views of this kind in isolation, they are an essential part of any screening process. If followed up by a trainer they can provide a very useful introduction to a thorough and more immediate discussion of training requirements.

THE BOSS'S VIEW OBTAINED BY INTERVIEW WITH A TRAINER OR MANAGEMENT ADVISOR

This can be carried out either as a follow up to a more formal reporting system or entirely separately. By providing the opportunity for more probing questions it does give an opportunity for the management development requirements of a whole section to be looked at and discussed in perspective. The boss also has an opportunity to give his views against the background of fuller information about the available training possibilities and the likely career possibilities within the company. This makes for a much more meaningful discussion. It is also a two-way training process, in that bosses can learn much more about the way people may be developed and the scope within their own particular area.

GROUP VIEW

Management development activities must affect a wide range of managers and groups within the company and there is a strong case for carrying out some of the background analysis in a formal review meeting. The terms of reference of such a group could be:

- to list the names of managers whose training and development should receive priority (normally managers thought to be ready for promotion within two years);

- to review the list every four months and report to the appropriate director;

- to review the list in the light of the current vacancy position and agree recommendations;

- to make recommendations for training and development.

Figure 8.1 illustrates how comments may be summarised and plans for agreed action finalised.

In terms of training needs analysis this kind of activity can be of value not only in pinpointing specific long-term training requirements but also in giving an opportunity for the discussion with representatives of key management areas of the short- and long-term problems to which training may contribute. For those organisations working to an ISO 9000 framework this could be part of 'Management Review'. The primary purpose of any structure of this kind is long-term development, but it can quickly lead to a clear recognition of the need for more detailed analysis related to present performance and more immediately related to the present operation. It will not be long before training prescribed for 'high flyers' has more relevance to a wide range of managers. In other words there is a need for 'management maintenance' as well as management development.

This will also lead to a recognition of the fact that although management development can to some extent be conducted on an individual basis, management training on a comprehensive basis must also be tackled from the group point of view. The learning problems of many operations will be seen as group problems related to group situations, The focus of all these operational problems will be at Board level where the whole range will come under scrutiny. As these problems are faced and thought through, the stage is set for really broadly-based operational reviews of management training and for the establishment of a comprehensive system of training based on the audit.

Figure 8.1   Summarised plans and finalised actions

NAME	AGE	JOB	YEARS IN JOB	GRADE	PREVIOUS COMMENTS	COMMENTS AND ACTION SINCE LAST MEETING
F Bishop	27	Depot sales supervisor	1¾	2	Developing well. Still has further potential. Head office experience to be considered early in 2009.	To attend field sales managers course July.
R Brown	23	Sales operations officer	1	1	Promising young man. To be considered for initial marketing background courses.	Attended initial marketing course.
D Gosling	37	Special accounts manager	¾	3	Developing well. Secondment to sales operations has provided useful experience. To return to district management 1 September. Nominated for management course.	Return to district management postponed. Attended managers' course October 2008.
H Hart	30	Operations analysis officer	1½	1	Could do a bigger job as a specialist. Progress to be reviewed at the technical development meeting. To take part in training discussion groups. Should be considered for project group training.	Has attended training discussion group. An extension of this training is being considered.
N Jordan	35	Assistant manager, marketing analysis	5½	1	Could do a bigger job as a specialist. Progress to be reviewed at the commercial development meeting. To take part in training discussion groups. Should be considered for project group training.	Appointment to management position January pending.
H Masters	24	Assistant Product manager	½	2	Probably has very high potential. Continues to make excellent progress. Upgrading to be considered at the end of the year. Nominated for accounts course and initial advertising course.	To be upgraded to higher management. Attended accounts course November.

Operational Analysis and Management Training

Although traditional approaches to management training and development can provide a starting point for an integrated training system, they are in this context a means to an end. The end is to achieve a full operational analysis as a foundation for management training. All the background work of education and development is vital but not necessarily the most important part of a total management training activity. A major problem now in companies is to unify approaches in the light of short- and long-term assessments of training needs.

In order to illustrate the process of really getting to the roots of a comprehensive appraisal of needs as the basis for a complete operational training programme, it is necessary to examine a wide range of approaches and 'trigger mechanisms' which may be of particular value to the internal training manager.

In this process the traditional distinctions between supervisory training, management training and management development will be seen to be virtually meaningless. From the operational point of view the trainer is concerned with various levels of management, some of which have traditionally been called supervision. The distinction is one of level not of kind and in learning and training terms cannot usefully be separated. Management development also ceases to be a useful term as a total short- and long-term training approach is developed. In some areas it has in any case only been used as a fashionable euphemistic term for management training.

WHERE TO START

The problem of starting a comprehensive top-level audit must be faced quickly. There is no one ideal approach but a number of basic tactics are reviewed as examples. The problem of describing the techniques involved in a training audit at this level is that there is no clear dividing line between analysis and remedy. The process is one of continuous evolution. Although in the first instance much basic information may be obtained from a review divorced from the situation, many activities will have a dual purpose of training and of diagnosing further problems. Inevitably, part of the training programme involves enabling managers to recognise and face up to problem situations. One aim must be to improve insight either in individual or group terms. Further insight will improve the effectiveness of the audit and ensure its constant modification. The system for continuous training needs analysis will be integrated with a continuous training process. The techniques described will, therefore, be in many cases basic training techniques, although here they will only be viewed from the analysis point of view.

MANAGEMENT DIAGNOSIS

The trainers must be able to call upon every diagnostic technique available to the management or organisation consultant. Before the potential and contribution of training techniques can be assessed they must be able to probe thoroughly the strengths and weaknesses both of the organisation as a whole and of the individual managers in it. The trainer must be highly trusted by management and must have access to a wide range of material. It is essential to sense the existing patterns of change in the organisation and those required for the future, and they must harness these to achieve the maximum in learning terms. There will be two main groups of problems, some new, some traditional.

MANAGER'S PROBLEMS

These may be individual or group problems related to:

- knowledge and skill;

- personal competence;

- preparation for promotion;

- adjustment to structural changes;

- personal relationships;

- authority and leadership;

- personal objectives.

ORGANISATIONAL PROBLEMS

These are problems which may not be discovered from initial discussions with managers but are highly relevant to the training situation:

- structure;

- integration;

- philosophy;

- company planning and objectives.

It is often difficult to make a sound analysis of real training needs in this area because of the confusion of symptoms and causes. Organisational ills will be analysed by some managers in terms of apparent failures in communication or inadequate understanding of systems such as 'Management by Objectives' and Key Performance Indicators (KPI's). Most organisations have now passed the stage at which such comments would lead straight to courses in communication techniques or the logic of integrated planning. The real problems, of which these are symptoms, are probably related to basic questions of structure or integration and are certainly not easy to assess.

AIMS OF ANALYSIS

To avoid superficial discussions of symptoms the aims of the analysis must be clearly defined. These aims will vary in different situations but may be on the following lines:

- to discover key strengths and weaknesses in the organisation and management team;

- to assess the direction of organisational development;

- to make an initial interpretation of these factors in learning and training terms;

- to analyse them in terms of the need to build a learning and training system into the organisation. This should provide for continuing reassessment of the problems and training needs and the establishment of a cycle of continuous retraining and management development.

How to Make the Analysis

The methods of analysis discussed earlier are not entirely adequate at management level because here the techniques of training and analysis must be integrated. A fuller and more specific review is, therefore, required. Important differences in emphasis can be seen in all the basic processes of asking questions in job and operational analysis, and the various techniques of group analysis assume greater importance.

ASKING THE PERSON

As at other levels, this must form a significant part of the process of analysis. It is especially difficult at the management level to distinguish degrees of training needs and to separate symptoms from causes.

ASKING THE BOSS

This part of the process is particularly significant when considering top-level management problems. The boss's own philosophies and beliefs are so important that a thorough analysis of them is essential and is likely to provide major clues to both problems and training needs.

JOB ANALYSIS

Thorough job analysis is again of great importance but must be kept clearly in line with its prime purpose in relation to the audit which is to:

- provide a basis for training targets;

- clarify the objectives of the job;

- examine links with other jobs and the total training environment.

OPERATIONAL ANALYSIS

At management level this must include a look both forwards and backwards in terms of time. Patterns of learning and problem development in previous years will give many pointers to necessary action. Most management teams will be found to have a learning pattern if not truly a learning curve. In tackling problems which are repeated there will be evidence of adjustment in terms of learning from mistakes and in other ways and there will be evidence of the repetition of mistakes. All this must be examined if the learning process of individuals and groups is to be accelerated and improved in future.

The forward look is just as important. Training is by no means just the correction of errors. It is concerned with removing learning barriers impeding the achievement of targets and objectives. The direction of development and change and the desired target for change form the 'bench marks' for the target for training.

Group Analysis

It is in this area that the clearly dual function of analysis and training emerges. In fact, the processes concerned may well have a purpose and validity independent of both. Every situation will require its own detailed adjustments but there are a number of key categories of approach:

ORGANISATION CONFERENCE

At some stage it is essential for the top management team to meet and review, possibly amongst other things, its basic objectives and training needs. A properly structured conference at this level can be of the utmost importance to the trainer. Several things can be achieved at once. Exchange of ideas can provide a unique view of training requirements and, if consensus is achieved, the essential top-level backing for a programme of training and change can be quickly established. The whole process will also, of course, be a training situation. Rethinking will mean relearning.

MANAGEMENT GROUP TRAINING SEMINAR

Group training techniques will frequently form part of a training or change programme designed to improve organisational effectiveness and group management performance. The aims of these sessions will include:

- the 'unfreezing' of the management situation;

- the provision of a common language for assessing management problems;

- the establishment of close personal relationships and frank exchanges of views;

- the general updating of management thinking;

- practice in team work.

All these factors will inevitably lead to a very full review of the training needs both of the group concerned and the total organisation environment. They involve a high degree of analysis alongside personal and group learning. The more 'structured' the approach the more likely is the seminar to concern itself with the discussion of particular training needs. Checklists such as that in Appendix 8a constantly require a redefinition of strengths and weaknesses and provide the framework for defining training needs as well as a trigger for action. Appendix 8a describes a particular one-week seminar and illustrates the integration of a continuous process of training and analysis.

The result of this kind of programme in terms of a training audit is:

- a clear recognition by all concerned of individual needs related to knowledge, attitudes and skill;

- an appreciation of the needs of the working group and their relation to individual needs;

- a cross-section of views about the needs of the organisation;

- examples of the interpretation of the situation in terms of training needs, for example: the real skill required in a negotiation to obtain the best results for the organisation rather than a sectional victory – avoiding the worst features of the 'rat race';

- recognition that, as a manager, training needs analysis starts with oneself and one's own working group, illustrating the true line management responsibility for training.

MANAGEMENT STUDY GROUP

A consultant-type survey within an organisation by a representative group of managers is a means of tackling training analysis as well as other problems.

Although this approach can be effective and appropriate there are drawbacks which in many cases have diminished its value. These are:

- the part-time nature of the exercise frequently leads to superficial treatment by the majority of those concerned;

- pressures in the organisation lead frequently either to ineffective compromises within the group or to easy 'shelving' after the group has reported. Initial terms of reference usually provide for the analysis but rarely for the executive follow up. Work in the context of an independent Standard can help to avoid some of these problems.

Other Sources of Training Information

Training audit information may come from a wide range of activities and the trainer must be aware of the possibilities and be involved in any aspect of the operation of the business that will yield training information.

APPRAISAL

Appraisal systems are of various kinds but are normally used for four main reasons:

- to assess the performance of managers in their present jobs;

- to identify those with above average potential who will require special training for the future;

- to encourage improved performance now and in the future;

- to make salary recommendations.

The first three are central to the trainer's job and must be part of any system needed to provide a basis for training activity. Although the control of management appraisal may be elsewhere in the human resources or management structure, trainers must exercise a major influence over the procedure. Appraisal is too often seen as a pure measuring exercise. The need to encourage and improve performance is often overlooked. This is a real training process. Unless the trainer is closely involved, the procedure can produce the wrong information with the idea of judging rather than developing.

SETTING IMPROVEMENT AND DEVELOPMENT TARGETS

All objective setting systems are closely linked with appraisal and are of concern to the trainer in so far as they are vehicles for improvement and the setting of improvement targets, rather than pure analysis and measurement. In other words, they have a great training value when they are part of the basic system of management. Their value to training is that they both set targets for improvement – training targets – and actually accelerate improvement. Objective setting systems can:

- simplify the job;

- provide a measure of performance;

- involve line managers in direct training;

- be built into the continuous system of the business so that they are self-operating;

- encourage flexibility and growth;

- provide the framework and in many cases the motivation for change which is essential to training in the management area.

It is clear from this that in the management area there is no one ideal formula for a training audit. There are many sources of information including techniques which are sometimes considered only as active training methods rather than tools for analysis. Taking stock of training at this level involves an examination of the whole of the organisation and its purpose. An audit of training is impossible without an audit of the complete organisation.

Appendix 8a: Illustration of the Integration of Training and Analysis

This is a report on a management seminar that differed from conventional forms of management training in that it was concerned not so much with individual development as with the achievement of total company effectiveness in a changing environment. Emphasis was on how individual efforts could be integrated so as to produce this effectiveness.

PROBLEMS GIVING RISE TO THE SEMINAR

Some company problems to which it was hoped that this type of training might contribute are:

- resistance to change despite apparent willingness to accept change;

- the reluctance of some managers to examine their own organisations and to check that their activity is of the most purposeful in company terms;

- destructive competitiveness in which individual or local interests are put before company interests – the 'rat race';

- a lack of candour between managers and their peers and between boss and subordinate. This can result in:

  a. failure to give helpful criticism;

  b. stifling of problems.

AIMS OF THE TRAINING

The aims given to the course members were:

- to explore the workings of groups and organisations;

- to explore the effectiveness of various managerial styles;

- to relate conclusions from (1) and (2) above to the company.

COURSE PROGRAMME

Twenty-two managers took part and worked in four groups, in which status, function and work location were mixed.

Throughout the programme the method used was that members worked in groups on various projects and then analysed the way in which their groups had operated. This analysis is the 'process analysis' referred to throughout the programme and it was done against the checklist given at the end of this Appendix. Bar charts were produced of process analysis.

SUNDAY EVENING

20:00	Introduction to the course
20:15	Introduction to exercise 'Compensation'
20:45	Group decisions
21:45	Process analysis

In exercise 'Compensation' the members of each group were asked to recommend salary increases for ten young engineers who had joined a company a year previously with equal qualifications but who had then performed to different standards and worked in different environments. The process analysis which followed the groups' decisions showed that each group was confident that it was working well – a normal result after the first exercise, but one which reflects a lack of honest self-criticism rather than effective team work.

MONDAY

09:00	Briefing for next stage of exercise 'Compensation'
09:15	Second group stage of exercise followed by role-play
11:00	Discussion and briefing for building project
11:15	Planning stage of building project
14:00	Carry out building project
14:15	Process analysis
15:00	Exchanged plans exercise
16:15	Discussions on planning
17:00	Herzberg and McClelland films

20:00   Prepare a report on the validity of Herzberg, McClelland and grid theories and their applicability

On Monday the role-play, in which individuals had to deal with complaints about the salary awards given, led to a discussion on objective setting and boss-subordinate relations.

The building project put the groups into competition with each other as to who could plan to build the model in the shortest time.

Writing reports on the Monday evening caused the groups to discuss in greater depth the theories which had been presented to them. The ensuing analysis showed that they were more aware of the problems of working together and related training needs.

TUESDAY

09:00   Process analysis

10:00   Allocation of points to report

11:00   Course discussion

11:15   Start of exercise 'Negotiation'

11:30   Preparation for Negotiation

14:00   Negotiation

15:00   Discussion of exercise and briefing of organisation culture exercise

16:30   Preparation of group reports on the company organisation, its nature and problems

20:00   Continue preparing report

The 'allocation of points to reports' was an exercise in which each person met someone from another group and allocated 100 points between the reports prepared by their respective groups. They were asked not to divide the points equally and to try to assess the reports objectively. What happened was a win-lose situation and this was used to illustrate the loss of objectivity which occurs when one's own brain child is compared with someone else's.

Exercise 'Negotiation' also created a win-lose situation in which negotiators spent time trying to beat the other opponent rather than achieve the real objective of the exercise which was to reach agreement quickly – again a common problem. At 15:00 a brief lecture was given to the course members in which it was explained:

1. That organisations involve relationships between:

    • boss and subordinate;

    • members of working groups;

    • one working group and another.

2. That the process analysis had been intended to enable managers to look at the problems of (*b*): that exercise 'Negotiation' and the 'allocation of points' was dealing with the relationships under (*c*) and that the role-play for exercise 'Compensation' the 'Grid Theory', and the Herzberg and McClelland films had been dealing with the problems of (*a*).

A discussion on the nature of these problems followed and managers were asked to bear this in mind in preparing the group reports on the company organisation during the evening.

WEDNESDAY

09:00   Exercise 'Change'

14:00   Exercise 'Objectives' with observers

20:00   Exercise 'Life Goals'

The morning was free from 10:00 though between then and 14:00 each group was asked to choose two members for secondment to another group.

In the afternoon one decision of exercise 'Objectives' was taken by 'reshuffled' groups. The general feeling was that the new members integrated well through the common pattern which had been set by the process analysis. The other four decisions in exercise 'Objectives' were taken with one group watching another at work and doing a process analysis on that group. The observed group's own process analysis of the same exercise was then compared with that given by the observers and there was considerable similarity.

In exercise 'Life Goals' each manager ranked one possible 'life goal' such as 'wealth,' 'prestige' and 'self-realisation' both as they applied personally and to all members of the group. The managers then compared their view of their own goals with their view of each other's. The exercise proved the extent to which we mistakenly assume that others have the same aims as ourselves. The exercise was a useful preliminary to the following day.

THURSDAY

09:00 to 16:00   Discussion of managerial styles of group members

19:00   Informal dinner with guests

The groups were left completely to themselves to discuss the managerial styles of each group member. It was clear that most course members felt that this was one of the most valuable exercises of the whole week. The discussion had, it seems, been frank.

FRIDAY

09:00   Process analysis

10:00   Review of course and discussion of organisation development

12:00   Course ends

The process analysis of the discussion of managerial styles suggested that the groups had achieved a very sound working basis.

The course finished with an explanation of how this was intended as the first stage of a two-part training operation. In the second part, which would take place after all managers had been through a similar seminar, the intention was that managers should be asked to look at their own working groups in the same way as they had examined the workings of the groups in which they had been for the course. This was seen as a continuous process of training needs analysis, objective setting and performance review. During the discussion, what emerged was the need, not so much to criticise the workings of other departments, as to examine critically the working of one's own piece of the organisation, to discuss it openly and to act on the results.

GROUP CHECKLIST

The process analysis consisted of distributing 100 points amongst the statements under each of the following six headings according to the group's performance.

1. Decisions

    a. decisions were well-considered, based on facts and reason, and were reached by a consensus in which everyone was free to present feelings and thoughts and have them listened to;

    b. decisions were forced by an individual or a majority;

    c. issues were compromised rather than reasoned out;

    d. some members backed down too easily from opinions which they believed to be right;

    e. some members failed to participate.

2. Objectives

    a. objectives were clearly understood and accepted and group members worked constructively towards these objectives;

    b. members were vying for power;

    c. members were trying to score points rather than progress the group;

    d. irrelevancies and frivolity crept in;

    e. there was quibbling over unimportant detail.

3.   Efficiency

   a. the group was efficient, used its resources to the full and showed itself capable of adapting to any new challenge;

   b. individual talents and knowledge were not properly used;

   c. time was not properly used;

   d. rigid attitudes were shown and members did not always listen to each other;

   e. important ideas and information emerged later than they should have done.

4.   System

   a. the group approached the problem systematically. A method of approach was quickly agreed and then adhered to unless deliberately changed. Alternatives were generated, identified and properly evaluated;

   b. there was little real agreement on the system being followed. Discussion strayed wildly;

   c. there was undue reluctance to take decisions;

   d. it was not always clear when a decision had been taken. Issues were reopened and no good reason and the argument 'went round in circles';

   e. there was failure to quickly recognise and evaluate alternative possibilities.

5.   Disputes

   a. points of disagreement were thrashed out logically until all parties were satisfied. Tempers were controlled and reason prevailed over emotion throughout;

b. keeping the peace was more important than getting the best decision;

c. people 'agreed to differ';

d. personal victory mattered more than getting the best solution;

e. tempers were lost.

6.   Frankness

a. group members were frank, open, tolerant, and confident of each other's sincerity;

b. there were cliques;

c. intolerance was shown;

d. people were afraid of hurting each other's feelings;

e. some members were unduly guarded.

9

Initial Requirements for Costing and Evaluating Training

Costing and evaluation of training in a business is important to managers requiring competent staff, to accountants seeking to give financial guidance to the business manager, and to training specialists seeking to carry out their training function in such a way as to ensure that it makes the best possible contribution to the profitability of the business.

The implementation of costing and evaluation can be difficult since the training and learning process is an integral part of the business: it cannot be isolated from the business environment and is to some extent dependent for its effectiveness on the collaboration of a large number of interdependent managers and staff. There is also the difficulty that the effectiveness of training is dependent to a large extent on the belief that it is effective. This belief leads to those attitudes in the business which show that it is profitable to learn and that managers want people to have the best opportunities to learn effectively and quickly. With this motivation as the driving force, a training operation can be more effective. There are a number of intangibles in costing and evaluation of training – but no more than in functions such as public relations, sales promotions, or research and development.

Cost of Learning and Cost of Training

It is important to recognise that the cost of learning is different from the cost of formal training. In any business there will be a cost of learning – the costs incurred when people who do not know, and cannot do, must acquire the skill and knowledge necessary to perform their jobs. Training means the organisation of learning opportunities and the provision of resources to enable effectively motivated people to learn quickly and well.

Any business must have people who have adequate knowledge and skill to apply this knowledge to meet the organisation's current and planned needs. It is possible to recruit people with some of the knowledge and some or all of the skills required. It is unlikely that any recruit will be ready-made for a particular business. At the very least there will be a need to acquire further knowledge about the organisation, that is, practices, products and markets.

The alternative to such ideal recruitment is for people to learn the necessary skills, acquire the needed knowledge, and discover the effective ways of behaving inside the organisation. This requires each individual to learn, first on joining the organisation, later on promotion or change of job; and to relearn when new knowledge is available, new skills required due to technological or other change, or as company or management policies are changed.

This learning is costly in real money terms:

- payment to learn, for example, make up pay to a minimum wage;

- material wasted as the learner practises;

- ineffective decisions leading to loss of profit or prestige.

And many other costs or loss of potential profits.

Among the many factors affecting the success of a business is the effective use of the human resource. This use will depend upon the level of skill acquired, the degree of applicable knowledge available, and the appropriateness of the attitudes adopted to the business objectives. If all these are learned well then the business will prosper – if they are learned badly the business will suffer.

There is therefore a cost of learning being incurred within every organisation. Usually this cost is disguised in the methods used to report financial results and it will often be extremely difficult to identify, but not impossible. There can be great confusion in this area because managers and accountants have not recognised this essential point – that the costs of learning are unavoidable, that they differ from the costs of formal training, and that training is only valuable if it reduces the costs of learning and raises the ultimate level of profitability.

Cost-Value Relationship

Knowledge of the learning process is now so well developed that, given a stated training requirement, it is usually possible to say clearly what would be the most effective combination of training methods. However, as with any service, the market of each training activity must be carefully studied. Certain types of training require capital investment in, for example, a training centre or a programme for e-training. Once an investment has been made there will almost certainly be a cost of maintenance of the resource that has been created.

If the need indicates a preferred method of training likely to incur capital and operating expenditure out of all proportion to the demand (the number to be trained) and this makes the cost of training excessive in relation to its value then some method less appropriate from a learning point of view may be chosen.

The art or science of the training specialist is to adopt those methods of training and learning which, in the particular situation, cost a good deal less than the value they will achieve in terms of reduced learning time, improved learning and higher performance.

Unfortunately, over the past few years there has been a spate of fashionable training techniques which will not stand up to close examination of the cost-value relationship as a measure of the results of such training. Equally unfortunately, where these have been adopted by organisations, few accountants have taken care to delineate the costs of learning or to measure the costs of training activities and the savings or profits derived therefrom.

There is great similarity between the training activity and other activities in business such as operations research, industrial relations or publicity. There is a point below which the ratio of value achieved to effort expended is small. Above a certain break-point this ratio increases enormously. It is therefore important in considering costs of training to examine the way in which the ratio of cost investment to learning and retention varies. It is a waste of money to break off the training effort below this point. Equally it is a waste of money to expend much effort in training beyond the point at which the skills, knowledge and attitudes are effectively established at a high level. In this respect training may be seen to be particularly akin to the advertising operation in a business.

Manager's Responsibility

If it is accepted that training is an integral part of the business, and if it is agreed that the process of learning is a continuous one, two things follow:

1. That the responsibility for training, and for examining its cost and usefulness, rests squarely with the managers of the business.

2. That the costs of running specialist training sections or centres may be easily recognisable but are caused by decisions made by the operating managers of the business.

It is therefore essential that any costing or evaluation should be related to the individual with the training need. Careful budgeting of the activities of training specialists is essential for control purposes but can be misleading if it leads to the view that the training specialist is responsible for training cost.

Evaluation

Evaluation of training has become the stalking-horse of many opponents of the development of training. The demand is made that it shall be 'proved that training pays'. It cannot always be proved that training pays. What can be shown is that changes in methods of learning have effects which can be measured, demonstrated, or which can be made the subject of evaluation by a collection of opinions.

Examples abound of situations where the introduction of effective training methods has resulted in direct cost saving, greater output or some other measurable effect. One such example is given in the Appendix to this chapter, but it must be emphasised that these can only relate to tasks the results of which are measurable in terms of:

*   learning time taken;

*   the output before and after, with and without the particular training process advocated;

- the other characteristics of the situation which can be seen and be shown either to have improved as a result of the training or have remained the same – for example, quality of the product, customer satisfaction.

Much training in industry and commerce cannot be measured in this way and must therefore be subjected to quite different evaluation methods, usually involving value judgements which are not quantifiable.

One of the major problems that arise, particularly in management and supervisor training, is that the value obtained from training will be directly proportional to the value placed upon it and the belief expressed in it by all concerned, especially by top management. It is a salutary experience to watch the growth and decline of an organisation's belief in a particular method of management training – and the consequent growth and decline of the value obtained from that training, irrespective of its intrinsic worth.

The following chapters aim to give managers, accountants and training specialists common ground for discussion on the costing and evaluation of the training operation which must take place in a business if the training function, however it is organised, is to take its rightful place as an integral part of the business operation.

There will be no attempt to explore the social value of recent developments in the training field, nor to deal with the saleable value added to an individual's abilities on account of effective training. Both of these topics are extremely important to the nation as a whole, and to each of us individually, Equally, surely problems arising from these two aspects must be faced by employers and managers. For example, if a person has been well trained within one firm they are obviously valuable to another firm which needs someone with their skill and knowledge. These topics are ignored solely in order to restrict the discussion to manageable proportions.

It is of fundamental importance to industry that training should be viewed objectively, applying the most appropriate costing techniques and questioning attitudes to be as sure as is possible that good value is being obtained from the time, money and effort expended.

Appendix 9a: Worked Example of Financial Benefits of Training

The management of a factory manufacturing a domestic product has recognised the need to improve the productivity of the assembly department. It is considering the introduction of an off-the-job operator training area although the present training arrangements provide for on-the-job training instruction for one week with no formal training course. In the absence of detailed records, discussion with the supervisors and operators reveals that the training time to reach the average operator performance on simple appliances is of the order of 13 weeks. The target of performance for the assembly operators is 100 on the BSI rating scale (Experienced Worker's Standard).

The analysis of present operator performance is shown in Figure 9.1 based on a period of one week, but reflects the performance of a period of 12 months. The maximum operator performance is about 120 for women and 130 for men, the minimum rating 45 and 75, respectively. Average operator performances on the various assembly lines vary between 74 and 105.

Figure 9.2 gives the cost of make-up to time rate and amounts to some £1,041 per annum.

The analysis of the labour turnover is given in Figure 9.3 and shows the breakdown of terminations over the past 12 months where some 80 per cent of the operators left during the period.

Thirty-six per cent of the operators left during their training period, the average length of service of this group was four weeks and none had reached bonus earnings.

Figure 9.1   Performance of operators

JOB OPERATOR	PERFORMANCE WOMEN			PERFORMANCE MEN		
	AVERAGE	MAX	MIN	AVERAGE	MAX	MIN
Line 1	83	92	45			
Line 2	80	92	75	95	130	91
Line 3	105	120	85	105	110	100
Line 4	94	110	85			
Line 5	85	103	78	85	105	75
Line 6	74	93	45			
Line 8	95	103	93			
Line 9	97	115	90			

Figure 9.2   Cost of make-up per week

LINE NUMBERS	WOMEN			MEN		
	NUMBER BELOW TIME RATE	NUMBER LESS THAN AVERAGE	COST OF MAKE-UP (£)	NUMBER BELOW TIME RATE	NUMBER LESS THAN AVERAGE	COST OF MAKE-UP
1	3	2	3.95			
2	1	4	0.26	0	2	
3	0	3	8.16	0	1	£0.26
4	2	3	0.11	1	6	
5	3	5	5.69			
6	6	6	1.28			
8	1	7	1.98			
9	2	3				

LOSS OF PRODUCTION AND COST

To determine the hours lost for each line in the assembly department, an example calculation is shown for Line 1 as follows:

From Line 1, Figure 9.2

The total number of operators below average performance = 5

From Line 1, Figure 9.1

The average performance = 83

Then the hours lost per week on Line 1:

$$= \frac{(100 - 83) \times 40 \times 5}{100} = 34$$

Where the target of performance is 100 on the BSI scale, based on a 40-hour week.

Figure 9.3   Analysis of terminations over previous year

JOB OPERATOR	NUMBER OF OPERATORS	LENGTH OF SERVICE				% TURNOVER OVER LAST TWELVE MONTHS	NUMBER LEFT IN TRAINING	NUMBER LEFT AFTER TRAINING
		UNDER 6 MONTHS	6–12 MONTHS	1–3 YEARS	OVER 3 YEARS			
Line 1	8	7		1		67	5	3
Line 2	3	2	1		2	27	2	1
Line 3	17	11	4	1	3	121	4	13
Line 4	4	4	1		1	45	4	9
Line 5	10	5	2	1	1	67	1	4
Line 6	9	7	1			75	5	4
Line 8	4	2				44	4	11
Line 9	15	8	5			300		

Tabulating the results for the calculation of hours lost for each line, as follows:

	HOURS LOST PER WEEK	
LINE NUMBER	WOMEN	MEN
1	34	
2	40	4
3		
4	12	
5	48	42
6	124.8	
8	16	
9	6	
Total	280.8	46

The cost of production is £5.00 per hour for women and £5.50 for men.

Then, the cost of production lost per year is:

for women
= 280.8 x 48 (hours) @ £5.00 per hour
= £67,392

for men
= 46 x 48 (hours) @ £5.50 per hour
= £12,144

TOTAL loss for department
= £79,536

COST OF PROPOSED SYSTEMATIC ANALYTICAL TRAINING

Estimated length of course   3 weeks

Number of trainees   70

Annual cost: (for first year of operation)

Trainee pay
= 70 x 3
= £9,975

Instructor pay   = £3,120

Operator training officer   = £8,000

Training area equipment   = £6,000

Running costs   = £3,950

TOTAL   = £31,045

POSSIBLE SAVINGS

		(or with only 75% of this loss)
Loss of production cost	= £79,910	£60,000
Present training cost	= £8,530	£8,530
TOTAL	= £88,440	£68,530
Cost of proposed training	= £30,845	£30,845
NET SAVING	= £57,595	£37,500

The total net saving will be in excess of £57,595 (£37,500) since the analysis takes no account of production work achieved in training and reflects the operator performance from the average rating to 100 rating.

10

Cost of Not Training

It is sometimes said that there are organisations with no training needs. If such cases exist the top manager of that business should be able to sign a declaration on the following lines:

Declaration from an Organisation Claiming to Have No Training Need

- We have taken on no newcomers to this business in the past year and predict that there will be no need to do so in the next two years.

- Each member of the staff workforce and management of this business is fully competent at their job and requires no further development to meet the needs of the business – now or within the known period of the planned activity of this business.

- This business is operating at the peak of efficiency and will continue to do so for the predictable future. There are fully trained people ready to take over any positions which might fall vacant in the next year due to premature retirement or ill health of any of the staff or management. We shall not need to recruit replacements for any consequent vacancies.

- There are no staff members of the business who are:

  a. under the age of 18 and doing work requiring the exercise of considerable knowledge and skill;

  b. indentured under any form of apprenticeship, articles or other form of agreement, written or understood, which implies that they will be trained for a craft, commercial or technical occupation.

- The growth rate and change in methods contemplated for this business are such as to require no retraining of staff or management in the foreseeable future.

- The market for the products of this business is such as to preclude any expansion requiring new management procedures, new organisation structures or the development of new techniques of selling or administration.

- Each member of the staff of this business is used to the full extent of their capacities and there is sufficient overlap of job knowledge and capability of performance as to give the flexibility required in the event of holidays, sickness or other absence.

- Relationships within this organisation – that is, between managers, supervisors and staff – are excellent and lead to no destructive conflict in the conduct of our affairs.

- We recognise that this state of affairs – leading as it does to a situation in which training is unnecessary – is unusual. If at any time conditions arise where any of the above statements are not true, we acknowledge that it is likely that a training need will arise – the fulfilment of which would assist in righting the situation.

- We recognise our social responsibility as employers to organise effective training and further education for our staff and management both to cope with the learning needs of the business and to promote job satisfaction for all employed by us.

It is difficult to envisage a manager able to honestly put their signature to such a declaration. Every business needs to train its workers and managers to ensure its continuing growth and prosperity. The cost of not training will be found in high staff turnover, low morale and failure to respond to changes in environment.

Recruitment and Staff Turnover

If a business recruits newcomers into its ranks it may do so at many levels, but, at every level of recruitment it must choose to recruit either:

- people already trained to a large extent;

- people with little or no relevant training.

In either of these cases, training will be needed to fit the newcomers to the governing features of the environment – probably by means of an induction process to accustom them to the procedures, regulations, and ways of thinking and behaviour operating in the business.

The recruitment of ready-trained staff is often illusory as a benefit to the business since there may be a retraining need which outweighs the advantage of avoiding job skill and knowledge training.

There is an argument that correlates the amount of training inversely to the rate of staff turnover and certainly it has been shown that good training can be effective in this way because:

- it is evidence of the organisation's real interest in the development of the newcomers;

- it overcomes the sense of inadequacy which may overwhelm a newcomer in the early stages of acquiring knowledge that is difficult to relate to ordinary experience, or of developing special, very complex manual or perceptual skills.

Cost of Staff Turnover

UNDERMANNED PLANT

Where turnover is high, two factors prevail:

1.   Recruitment can rarely keep pace with the actual numbers who leave and frequently there are a few days or weeks during which the operation is undermanned and is not producing at the rated

capacity – certainly not at the capacity envisaged when the capital was invested in it.

2.   Even when all leavers have been replaced the new operators will probably not be as skilled and the plant will still be working below capacity.

Direct cost: Lower than expected return on capital investment.

RECRUITMENT

Those who leave have to be replaced. There may seem to be plenty of local potential employees but, if turnover is high, things may not turn out as expected. So there has to be a recruiting drive.

Direct costs:

- notices and advertisements;

- telephone calls to the job centre;

- telephone calls;

- a proportion of overheads;

- visits to local schools and so on;

- television space and so on.

SELECTION

The company that does no selection and therefore has no selection expenditure, will soon have no selection to do and will have to take on anybody who comes along. This situation is usually the precursor of an even higher labour turnover.

Selection costs might include:

- letters arranging interviews;

- interview time and overheads;

- selection test costs and so on;

- health check costs;

- interview costs;

- correspondence and so on.

LEARNING

Any form of learning costs money. Often the least expensive is the most easily identified.

EXPERIENCE

The costs of gaining experience are those most widely overlooked. They are of course an extension of those very high costs (and risks) incurred in on-the-job training. Some of the principal areas may be identified under the following headings:

- 'overpayment';

- learning costs;

- reduced utilisation of capital equipment;

- damage to plant;

- strain on plant resulting in latent defects;

- closer supervision requirement;

- making good poor workmanship;

- actual breakage and wastage;

- delayed delivery – loss of goodwill and costs of delay – penalty clauses;

- customer complaints on quality and so on;

- team morale – not meeting targets, outputs, bonuses, and so on;

- accidents – lost time, under-manning, compensation, litigation, prosecution.

However well people are trained on a course or in a training centre, they will require a period of gaining experience and some of these costs may be incurred; closer supervision and tuition is required although the more serious items such as major damage to plant may be avoided. But if a newcomer is thrown in at the deep end many more of these expenses are likely to be incurred.

MOTIVATION

This overlaps other issues. A team constantly dragging along one or more people who do not have sufficient experience will find it difficult to meet the expected performance (be this implicit or assumed) and the morale of the team will fall even when there is no direct effect on wage packets. This will be particularly true if output is maintained by some having to work harder than expected in order to cover for the inefficiencies of the new starters. Once motivation slips in this way new starters will be made to feel unwelcome – they will be ridiculed for their ineptitude – will not be helped or advised – will soon feel incapable and 'in danger' and will leave. The process will start again with the next new starter and the old hands will feel more depressed.

There is, however, an interesting apparent contradiction which whilst not directly relevant to the costing of turnover should be mentioned. Where a group has a trainee attached to them on the right basis, this can boost the morale of the team. If they are made responsible for administering the training programme, made responsible for seeing the trainee is *trained* they will give every assistance, they will give encouragement – they will not feel in danger or inept and will learn more and more quickly. It depends entirely on how the trainee and the training is introduced to the group. If the group is chosen because it is the best group of trainers and this is made known, the kudos and responsibility will increase motivation despite any reasonable pressure put on them to achieve an output.

Motivation is difficult to cost, except in terms of its direct impact on overall turnover, but it can be measured (Herzberg, 1968).

PUBLIC IMAGE

This is a significant factor in the cost of employee turnover. A company with a known high turnover will not be able to attract the type of people it wants or the type of worker who will stay with it.

Similarly, the self-respecting job centre will not, where there is any choice, send its better people to companies known to have a high turnover.

There are two other marginal factors. The public image engendered to high turnover is one of instability. Where such instability is suspected it can have an influence upon contracts, credit, bank loans and capital investment. Even if these facilities are not withheld it may mean increased effort in terms of time, wages, support and publicity to convince people that they can rely on the organisation's ability to meet its commitments.

PLANNING

Most of the key issues can be summarised under this heading. If the organisation cannot control who will leave and when – if it cannot control its ability to have available the skilled personnel it needs – then it cannot fully control its commitments or its ability to meet them. It cannot plan. It cannot optimise the use of its people, its capital, its buildings and its plant. It will, without planning, inevitably overstretch in some areas and it will then have to indulge in costly fire-fighting exercises even if this is only excessive overtime to meet a deadline. It will certainly under-utilise other elements, it will not get the expected return on investment and although this will be seen in a lower profit than expected, that profit reduction should also be seen, in part at least, as a cost of turnover.

Operational Needs

In any business there will be bottlenecks which restrict output or sales, and areas of low efficiency which affect the profit-earning capacity of the business. Often these areas of low efficiency are not recognised until an analysis is made, and it is interesting that, frequently, training surveys will throw up the existence of such areas in a clear way. It is obviously beneficial to the business to eliminate bottlenecks and to raise efficiency. There are several methods of overcoming such problems: mechanisation, redesign of product or change of materials. However, it might well be that effectively organised training can lead to the same result, and often at a lower cost, than the purchase of expensive machinery and retooling for new designs.

Every business suffers from its staff being absent for one reason or another, and from losses of fully trained people unexpectedly. This means that, apart from doing an effective job, individuals need to learn how to do other jobs in order to be available as substitutes during the absence of colleagues and the need to prepare for promotion and stop-gap appointments. Untrained people are a common source of inefficiency in industry, and there is therefore a learning need for people to prepare in advance of the occurrence. This is made difficult from a training point of view because such learning is likely to be ineffective unless the learner has an opportunity to exercise new-found skill and knowledge within a reasonable time of its acquisition.

Social Responsibilities

Organisations have a real responsibility towards young people up to the age of 18 years, to ensure that they are given opportunities to develop as individuals and to acquire considerable knowledge and skill. Learning at this age is relatively easy and the cost of training then makes for good investment. If a learner stays with the firm beyond the age of 18 it can be shown that great benefits can accrue from an investment of this kind.

Employers have a social responsibility to their employees in terms of job satisfaction and have the problem of effectively relating job satisfaction with job utility. This creates the need for people to be able not only to do the task assigned to them, but to understand why it has to be done, why it has to be done in the way prescribed, and its contribution to the ultimate purpose of the business. At the same time it is important for every business to capitalise on the innovative qualities of its entire staff, and to offer opportunities for them to contribute their ideas to the development of the business. Such attitudes are, of course, developed only by creating an atmosphere in which this type of thinking, this inventiveness, is profitable to the individual, not only in terms of monetary rewards such as payments for innovation, but in reputation and appreciation within the group.

Business Environment

Businesses respond to their environment and change accordingly. If they do not it is likely that they will fail. The market for the products of a business is the dominating feature which will determine new management procedures, new organisation structures, new techniques of selling, new demands on production research and development. Workpeople and management who have been successful in the past may find themselves inadequate to the challenge of the new situation and may face the extremely difficult learning situation of discarding a previously successful approach and adopting a novel approach in the new situation.

A business that is growing will need extra staff or, alternatively, if it is using more mechanisation it will require more skilled employees in the form of technicians who will need to learn about the new methods to be used. At the same time the existing staff and management will need to be retrained for this purpose. Many new methods and ways of operating have failed in the past not because they were intrinsically bad, but because the individuals required to operate them had not learned the effective methods required. There is therefore a great need for training for new skills in a growth situation and a retraining need for the present employees.

A business needs to have sufficient flexibility to cope with variations in its activity cost caused by outside factors, for example the seasonal effect on ice-cream manufacture. To be able to cope with this it is essential to have a sufficient overlap between the acquired skill and knowledge of individuals so that in such situations the business can be effectively staffed.

Structure of the Work Force

Since every organisation has a social group structure, containing within it a number of interrelated sub-groups, which are constantly changing, there is the need within each business for an effective method of communication, an objective attitude to collaboration with others, and generally what might be called 'good human relations'. This is not to say that there should be no conflict within a firm, but rather that such conflict should not prevent the firm attaining its objectives. To achieve such effective relationships it is important that everyone in it should be able to communicate using the right techniques capably and well, and having the right attitude to others. Training in the skills of communication and effective relationships is at a very early stage of development, but is of fundamental importance to any successful business.

An organisation must, in assessing its training needs, consider the age structure of the business, the possibility of retirement, sickness and death, and have a plan for succession. This plan for succession will be meaningless unless there is a corresponding training plan for the people concerned.

Assessing Training Needs

Techniques for establishing training needs are reviewed in Chapter 4. The process of assessment may be done internally but a different or, possibly, more objective review may be undertaken by consultants. The ideal would seem to be the use of outside help and advice to pose the questions, and the involvement of the management and staff of the business in answering the questions and deducing the consequent training needs. This has been done over the last few years by many firms. Emas Consultants have worked in this area since 1971. There is considerable evidence that such analysis leads not only to effective training operation but also to the revelation of other ways of improving business performance which have not been seen before. Certainly where skills analysis procedures have been applied to jobs, the methods used in those jobs have frequently been challenged and changed to give more effective operation, quite apart from the improvement derived from training.

Whenever an assessment is made it is essential to keep everyone in the company informed about the assessment process from a very early stage. This will go a long way toward establishing the right attitude and will lay a firm foundation for eventual acceptance of responsibility for systematic training. Full documentation is also essential at every stage of the assessment. All information should be carefully and immediately recorded.

The following summary indicates the form of a complete assessment of an organisation's training needs.

The following assessment review was compiled by C.D. Ellis in the first edition of our book *Analysis and Costing of Company Training*. It complements Chapter 4.

First Phase of the Assessment

FACTORS IN THE BALANCE

In the first phase, a series of fairly broad questions should be raised concerning the present situation and the predicted future of:

- The work environment: the aims and objectives of the company; its policies, the effectiveness of its major work areas (finance, production, marketing and sales, HR).

- The workforce and its ability to meet this present situation and future plans.

These factors must be balances. Discrepancies between the existing situation and defined objectives will indicate where action is required to effect change. Changes may be required in work methods; or to ensure that the right number of people with the right skill, knowledge or attitudes are available to meet present or future circumstances. The problem may be one of management organisation or administration, for example, departmental organisation, discipline and job methods. Or it may be a problem for which systematic training is the right answer.

At this stage the following questions will be asked.

QUESTIONS ABOUT THE ORGANISATION

- What are its overall aims and objectives? Are changes anticipated?

- What are its total resources and market potential?

- Is the organisation good enough to achieve its objectives?

- Is it really profitable?

- How can it be improved?

- What changes are likely to occur in its ownership, in rationalisation of its products, or its markets?

QUESTIONS ABOUT FINANCE

- Are the financial resources used as effectively as possible?

- Is adequate provision made for deployment of capital in terms of investment in research, development and production?

- Is budgeting effective?

- Is cost forecasting and cost control effective?

- Are we qualified to answer these questions?

QUESTIONS ABOUT PRODUCTION

- Is there any difficulty in maintaining consistency and/or quality of output?

- Have adequate precautions been taken to provide alternative production capacity?

QUESTIONS ABOUT MARKETING AND SALES

- What is the record of sales activity?

- Are sales and production geared together satisfactorily?

- Is our selling carried out most effectively and economically?

- Is the coverage of our markets adequate?

- What are the complaints levelled against sales staff? (For example, promptness of delivery, failure to reach specification, inability to meet competition.)

QUESTIONS ABOUT THE PLANT AND MACHINERY

- How good is it and can it be improved?

- Can it be run, controlled or maintained better?

- Can this be done by improving the quality of the supervisors, operatives or fitters?

- Or is capital investment the only answer?

- What future changes are likely, that is, developments requiring new machines?

- Are new standards likely to be harder to maintain?

- Are completely new systems of control likely to take over from older methods?

- And does this mean a much higher quality of machinists or maintenance specialists?

QUESTIONS ABOUT THE PRODUCT

- Are there too many sub-standard items that have to be discarded?

- Are there customer complaints?

- Is the internal inspection too lax or too stringent or inconsistent?

- What sort of competition will there be in the future?

- Should the firm withdraw from a particular field or specialise in it?

- Is it good enough; or is it above needed specifications, involving excessive cost?

- Can it be improved or made at lower cost?

- Is pricing competitive?

- Are sizes likely to change to metric?

- Are new products likely or possible?

- Can the old-fashioned line be replaced by a more efficient and economical new one?

- Is there a high degree of waste or breakage?

QUESTIONS ABOUT OUR WORKFORCE

- How good are they as a team and individually?

- How have they been trained and developed to date?

- Can their efficiency and performance be improved?

- Are they versatile and able to tackle more than one job?

- Are more needed in any particular sector?

- Are there a number approaching retirement age?

- Is there a recruitment problem? Are young people being attracted?

- Is there job satisfaction?

- Is there a turnover problem?

- Are the right people doing the right jobs?

- Are managers, supervisors and instructors trained to train others?

- How does the area where the factory is situated affect the employment position?

- Is there ready availability of people of all the necessary skills and educational requirements?

- Is there a shortage in any category?

- Are there other influences in the district which could attract people away from the firm?

- Is it a development area or is it an area into which new businesses are already coming?

- Will this cause a shortage or increase the rate of turnover?

Answers to these questions may give certain broad pointers to training requirements. If changes are radical, it may be that top management needs to develop knowledge of new control techniques. Newly recruited specialists may need to be trained in the organisation's philosophy. Individual jobs may expand or contract and their holders should be trained to meet this situation before pressures have really built up. Even if no change is envisaged, an enquiry into the pattern of personnel organisation and individual job performance may reveal areas where there is room for improvement. In many small businesses there is a very real need for appreciation of production and methods control. Value analysis and costing techniques may be found to be rather formidable to the managing director of a very small company; an elementary knowledge of exactly this subject might be the factor which will keep his business going.

Second Phase of the Assessment

The first phase of the assessment process, which will have helped to identify general problem areas, should be followed by a more detailed assessment of training needs. This second stage will establish clearly who needs to be trained; in what order of priority; how many need to be trained in each employee category; and to what standards of performance.

It may be profitable to consider seriously whether to employ an outside specialist for this more detailed work.

Recording of information becomes particularly important at this stage. Most managers could express an opinion about the efficiency of a machine, of a service or of a person, but unless these opinions are recorded, it is extremely difficult to relate one to the other and reach a solution which does not create yet another problem. The manager's knowledge needs to be ordered and made clear enough to form the basis of a more concrete plan. Writing it down and then discussing it with colleagues is a simple, effective way of doing this. It will lead to the formulation of training plans for the individual, and will provide evidence against which progress can be measured subsequently.

METHODS

A combination of methods is often used for this phase. Those available range from the simple note to the most sophisticated current practices. An outline of the principal methods is given below.

- Performance appraisal – a systematic approach to spot the gaps between existing and required job performance. This will indicate individual and group needs, and allow for the planning of tailored training programmes.

- Management query – asking managers for their opinions on training priorities (a useful supplement to more objective sources of information).

- Opinion surveys – a questionnaire about the value of different training approaches. A questionnaire leading to an analysis of the difference between the manager's and the job holder's conception of the job.

- Observation – either of a general nature (accident hazards, communication, poor maintenance and so on); or more specific (a particular work category or critical area of activity).

- Leaving interviews – for analysis of reasons for turnover and so on.

- Analysis of personnel changes – to anticipate changes in production, machines and so on.

- Analysis of personnel statistics – close study of turnover, age distribution, absenteeism, grievances, accidents.

- Analysis of supervisory problems.

- Analysis of in-plant production costs.

COMPLETING THE PICTURE

By the end of this second stage, a fairly complete picture of the distribution of the workforce should have been built up. Shown on an organisation chart in terms of job category (management, supervisory, technician and so on), of age, and so on, this will throw up natural lines of promotion; and will also show areas where recruitment is likely to become necessary. This should be studied, together with the following additional data:

- A departmental analysis of turnover to plan recruitment and highlight problem areas.

- Forward information about production plans.

- Assessments of present performance to find out if existing training arrangements are resulting in the desired standard within the desired period of time.

- An analysis of product quality – of wastage and customer complaints.

Third Phase of the Assessment

The first phase of the assessment process was diagnostic: it revealed the problems. The second stage was analytical: it identified the areas of greater importance. The third stage consists of taking action on the information gained and will lead to a pattern for the organisation's immediate and future training policy. This, in turn, will help to decide whether or not it can carry out training policies without outside help, where the immediate priorities for action lie, and what facilities should be created for meeting, controlling and assisting this action.

11

Cost-Value Relationship in Training

When considering any training activity, attention must be paid to certain factors if a decision is to be made that will result in the most profitable outcome. These factors are:

- the priorities for training;

- the suitability of employees for their jobs;

- the impact on management;

- the choice of training method.

Priorities

The Chapter 10 and Chapter 4 have shown how the training needs of an organisation can be identified. Any assessment should attempt to predict where the greatest return will result from an increase in training activity. Usually it is most profitable to apply the training effort to the area where learning need is greatest. This may simply be where the numbers to be trained are greatest and can be identified by considering growth rate, turnover and expected reorganisation caused by changes in the market, the technology of the business, mechanisation or the structure of management.

There are many who insist that the first priority in any business is the training and development of the present and potential managers of the business. They argue that without competent management giving its support on the basis of effective management learning and practices, any other training is bound to be less effective that it should be.

This view is logical but is not necessarily universally true. There are many businesses which have seen the supervisor as the key person in the training situation. These argue that, not only are the supervisors the link in the communication system of the business, but also that their acceptance of responsibility for the training of staff is vital to the operation of the business.

Yet again, there are those who advocate that, in industries where the technology and methods of working are changing rapidly, the training of technical staff is of prime importance.

What is the time factor in the situation? Should training be aimed at remedying the present lack of knowledge and skill or should it be concentrated on building a new cadre of well-qualified competent staff operating at a quite different level and possibly using quite different methods from those of the present set-up?

The age-structure and previous experience of the present staff will need to be considered and some estimate made of the rate of change occurring within the business and in the environment in which it operates.

If we take marketing as an example it may well be decided that, with increasing competition or some fundamental changes, in the characteristics of the outlets for products, a completely new marketing policy is required.

Would the business get better value from retraining the managers and staff operating the current policy or would more value be obtained by recruiting and training a new breed of marketing specialists unhampered by methods which, although successful in the past, are now irrelevant? The answer in most cases is almost certain to be a compromise since it is likely that no new policy will effectively be carried out unless understood by all concerned.

The Employee and the Job

The cost of training depends on the match between the individual's latent capacities and the job requirement and can be reduced either by recruiting better qualified staff or reducing the complexity of the job. Where neither of these is possible the training need may be greatest and long-term investment in such training – most probably combined with an educational process to supplement previous education and to complement the practical training – may be justified.

For example, it happens often that with automation a number of jobs arise, which are unlikely to appeal to those with an academic background but which require an understanding of the varying relationships of a number of factors in the situation, and the skill to make those adjustments which will put the situation back into balance if it drifts from normal. The operation of any furnace, kiln or oven is likely to have this characteristic.

Sales assistants in retail stores may be cited as another example. In this case, the whole success of the store may depend upon the ability to sell – a complex operation requiring high levels of skill in perception, communication and what might be called 'applied psychology'.

Are the skills and knowledge required special to the jobs in the business or are they the skills and knowledge which anybody in our culture would be likely to use in their ordinary working life?

If they are special, for example, require extremely fine hand and eye coordination, then it is probable that the learning will be greatly assisted by well-designed training, possibly working through special devices aimed at a swift progressive development of the skill needed.

If, on the other hand, the job demands little more than any man or woman can and does normally do, then the value of any extensive training may be very small indeed. This is probably true of some routine clerical operations – though not of all. Computer skills may be of a high order, as are many other clerical tasks. There seems no doubt that most offices would obtain very considerable savings through the application of simple but effectively designed training schemes. Savings of more than 15 per cent of total clerical cost could easily be achieved in most cases, with a much improved performance in terms of accuracy and speed flow of information.

Sacrifices by Management

How much present advantage in terms of output and activity is the management prepared to sacrifice in order to reap the advantage of effective training in the long term?

All training takes time and will, initially at least, reduce the availability of staff for production or other business activity.

For training of any kind there is a minimum period of time (varying with the individual) in which the learning is absorbed, assimilated and retained in such a way as to be capable of recall on demand.

To attempt effective training in less than this minimum time is to waste money. Unless the breakthrough point is reached and the learning established in the mind of the learner it will be quickly forgotten or, even worse, perverted and distorted in ways which would damage the business.

Opportunities to practise a new-found skill and knowledge or to appreciate the value of a new attitude are essential if basic learning is to be built upon to result in high performance.

The problem is to equate the obvious present cost of training in terms of lost production or other profit-earning potential with the value to be gained in the future from the investment.

In many instances, when examining programmes of training, it has been clear that the stated objectives of the programme (that is, the expected increase in value from the training activity) have been completely at variance with the time to be made available for the training. Much depends on the skilled definition of learning objectives.

It is not unusual for trainers to be told 'I want you to put on a programme for the supervisors. They need to communicate better, know more about cost control, be able to deal with the trade unions more firmly, raise the standards of quality, cooperate with the quality control department better and – of course – be better at dealing with people. You can have them one day a week for six weeks.' In such cases the training specialist should tell the manager that the extra value expected from supervisors cannot be obtained by this method or in this time. This is creating a present cost of training without considering whether it is likely to give value for money.

There is, of course, the other extreme where lengthy schemes of training are prepared which allow much more time than is needed for effective learning, resulting in greatly reduced motivation of the learner. Generalising dangerously, this is true of most schemes for the training and development of graduates – sometimes spread over two or three years during which the trainee has no opportunity to practise new-found skills or to test behaviour in the business situation.

Choosing the Right Training Method

No scheme of training will contribute to profitability unless the training itself effectively caters for the learning needs. The preparation of effective training programmes involves a knowledge of the business and its technology, a knowledge of people's reactions to given situations and expertise in the technology of training. Training is a developing subject which is steadily shedding its folklore and becoming, through ever-increasing research and investigation, an exact science. Unfortunately, the generalised development of the HR function has often slowed down this development and undervalued the training profession and its specialised skills. Perhaps there is a need to revitalise the profession. Some will say that the rot set in in the 1980s when public support for the Training of Trainers was abruptly withdrawn. It is sad that in much 'professional' training amounts to the selling of courses run by instructors selling knowledge rather than developing skills. Promoting profitable learning is not that easy. It should be a profession in its own right.

This is such a significant development that it is essential in any business to have the services of an expert training specialist.

If the training needs of a firm, now and in the future, are large enough, it will want to appoint its own training officers. This will mean an added continuing cost to the running of the business and it must be clear from the size and nature of the training problems that they will be employed sufficiently to accumulate value from their employment.

If the size of the problem does not warrant the employment of a full-time training expert, the business can share an expert's services with other companies using consultants.

The size of the training problem and, in particular, the numbers involved, will also determine whether a permanent training centre should be established and full-time instructors appointed. If these costs are not justified then external training courses will probably be used, but with caution.

The present plethora of general training courses placed on offer by a legion of societies, associations, colleges, institutions, consultants and individuals, is a measure of the lack of attention to individual and specific job training needs. This is particularly true in the field of training for management and supervisors.

Unfortunately a very large number of those responsible for making decisions about training rely upon the external course almost entirely, without reference to management standards. In consequence, find themselves perplexed to choose between the multitude of courses offered to them. The aims of such courses are usually accompanied by a long list of users (who may have only ever sent one person on the course) – and are stated in such general terms as to cover a multitude of possible training needs.

It is suggested that organisations would find it of advantage, in dealing with the problem of choosing appropriate external courses for their staff, to:

- limit their consideration to a small number of bodies providing courses – say up to a dozen;

- make effective liaison with these bodies so as to ensure that the true aims and methods of the courses are known and that the course is adapted to suit their needs in learning terms;

- consult with a reputable organisation that has information about other available courses when a need arises which cannot be met by the chosen disciples.

Too much money is wasted on sending staff and management on courses without proper consideration of the individual's real requirement for such a course, without preparatory briefing and without any effective in-company follow up to consolidate and utilise the learning.

A checklist of points to consider when choosing external courses is given in Appendix 11a.

Appendix 11a: Points to Consider When Choosing an External Course

1. THE FIRM'S REQUIREMENTS

- *Orientation.* The extent to which the course must be tailored to the organisations' requirements.

- *Timing and duration.* The time limit within which the course must be available; its duration and the length of time the organisation is prepared for the trainee to be away from work.

- *Cost.* The amount the organisation is prepared to pay for this particular training need.

- *Location.* Geographical limits, if any, on where the course may be held.

- *Impartiality.* Limits, if any, on the type of organisation providing the course, for example, universities, professional associations, management consultants.

2. THE COURSE

Within the context of the firm's own requirements, the following questions should be considered about the course:

- *Aims.* What the course hopes to achieve: whether the aims are explicit or implicit: realistic and achievable; sufficiently specific to enable the company to judge after the end of the course whether they have been achieved.

- *Content.* Should show expression of the aims of the course; logical progression of subject matter; correct balance within the time allocated.

- *Preparation and planning.* The care with which the course has been publicised; with which entry requirement for members has been worked out (some indication of level of work necessary); with which selection procedures are specified; and the reason for the course coming into being – was it to serve a real need or at industry's request?

- *Staff.* Their qualities, academic qualifications, business management experience (for example, on a consultant basis), their expertise.

- *Training methods.* Are these appropriate to the nature of the course; does the organisation want evidence of trainee participation by syndicate methods, and so on?

3. COURSE-ORGANISING BODY

Some aspects of the course-organising body may also need to be considered:

- *Its policies.* How it came into being; the place in its programme of business-management courses.

- *Its government.* Degree of autonomy and scope for initiative and flexibility.

- *Its growth.* Rapid growth may indicate adaptability, vigorous and dynamic leadership.

- *Emphasis on business management courses.* If these are only a small part of the curriculum, the previous criterion may be misleading.

- *Success of similar courses run by the organisation.*

- *Experimental or established course.* Companies may prefer to feel that they are sending trainees on a course which has been established sufficiently long to overcome its initial teething troubles.

- *Standing of the provider.*

- *Support.* Does the firm prefer a course which has local or national support; what is the status of other course members?

- *Approval.* Has the course had approval conferred on it by any official body; and if so, what is the standing of this body?

- *Facilities.* Are the surroundings and physical conditions adequate?

- *Follow-up.* Is there any follow up by the organising body, either by a follow-up course, or by contact with individual course members?

- *Interim liaison.* Readiness of the organising body to provide reports on trainees while the course is still in progress.

- *Frequency.* The frequency of a course may be an important factor where a number of people have the same training need and cannot all be released at the same time.

Further details about these criteria will be found in the article by John Nelson listed in the bibliography.

12

How Training Costs are Caused and Recorded

Training costs are defined as the total monetary investment made by an organisation as a result of the training function. They are the sum of all increases in expenditure and all decreases in income which stem from the decisions which management have taken about the training activity.

It is impossible to obtain a completely accurate picture of total training cost since many of the items will be so interwoven with other causes as to make it impossible to decide where a decision about training has affected cost.

The questions that must be asked are:

- What are the training costs?

- How are they caused?

- How valuable is it to record each type of training cost?

For comparison purposes training costs are often expressed as a percentage of payroll. Anything over 1 per cent is seen as a reasonable minimum. The biggest investors are likely to spend about 10 per cent. Certainly these organisations are taking training seriously and can demonstrate trading and market benefits.

There is the usual costing problem of distinguishing between:

- Direct costs incurred because an individual is being trained – expenditure which could be avoided if no training was done.

- Indirect costs which arise because resources are provided for the training operation and must be maintained if the facility for training is to be continued. If, in the short term, no training is done, these costs will continue until a new policy decision is made. These can be regarded as a consequence of policy and could be renamed training policy costs.

- Costs which arise because the firm exists and employs people, trained or untrained plans and organises its activities, provides resources and accounts for its performance.

- Opportunity costs, that is monetary sacrifice involved in employing capital in the training operation which could have been used in some other way.

From an accounting view of the business as a whole, all training costs will be regarded as indirect costs since they do not relate directly to adding value to the products or services of the company and they may be treated in two ways. Generally, cost of training is treated as overhead in the year that it arises, but in some cases – such as in training pilots on a new aircraft – it may be capitalised and written off over a period of years. Where costs are capitalised, the depreciation or amount written off will appear as a current cost.

Cost of Employing a Trainee

The direct costs of employing any trainee include:

- wage or salary paid;

- national insurance paid for the employer;

- pension fund contributions;

- other benefits;

- the costs of administering HR and training records, preparation of wages and other activities following on the employment.

These costs are caused by the basic decision to train the individual within the organisation rather than recruit staff who are already trained.

Such costs can easily be recognised where the trainee is being trained off-the-job, inside the organisation or at an external course. It is much more difficult to assess what part of such costs should be attributed to training when the training is being done on-the-job and results in some saleable product or contributes to the performance of a department.

However, even with on-the-job training, a reasonably accurate estimate can be made if the length of time taken to reach the expected standard of performance is known, the pay structure for trainees is known, and there are sufficient numbers of trainees to justify keeping the necessary records.

The extra cost of pay analysis to discern the first four items listed above for off-the-job training would not be great. In some cases it may even be worthwhile to accumulate these costs for trainees during their on-the-job training period and then apply an estimated percentage (representing the training time as a portion of the whole) to this total.

Whatever method is adopted, it is clear that these costs are affected by the time the trainee spends in developing skills and knowledge sufficient for the job. Whether practice on-the-job to reach the expected standards of performance can be regarded as training is a difficult question. If such practice is regarded as training then there may be, for a few types of work, a measure of this cost in terms of 'make-up' – that is, the amount required to bring the trainee's pay up to a certain level after taking into account the value of good production, sales made or other measurable activity.

In any event, since time spent on training is the cause of these costs, it is clear that any reduction in time spent to reach expected standards of performance in quantity and quality must reduce the cost of training. It is also true that most of this can be categorised as investment in people, but arguments about definitions are not very productive.

Providing the Means to Learn

The costs of providing the trainee with the means to learn divide naturally into two parts:

- external training costs;

- internal training costs.

EXTERNAL TRAINING COSTS

These are easy to define and collect. They consist of the following items:

- fees paid to the organisation providing the training;

- travel and accommodation expenses paid to trainees;

- books, stationery and examination fees.

It is probable that the ease with which these costs can be recognised has led to an emphasis in current thinking about training on courses run by external bodies such as colleges, private institutions and consultants. The simplicity of ascertaining external training costs is, however, offset by the extreme difficulty in many cases of assessing the value of the course. Many general courses are attended by thousands of people without any attempt at evaluation except the misleading collection of opinions from students at the concluding session.

Tests and examinations at the end of a course can be very deceptive and unduly academic. Training and education are not the same thing. Success or failure in an academic test may not necessarily be related to the practical learning and behaviour an organisation may be expecting. Hence the need for defining behavioural rather than academic objectives. Training is concerned with what people can do. Some public training courses are more concerned with teaching a particular syllabus that is useless in practice.

INTERNAL TRAINING COSTS

These are more difficult to assess than external training costs. The problem is simplest when the training is done at a training centre and only by full-time instructors. The costs in such a case may be itemised as follows:

Cost of the training centre consisting of:

- general and water rates;

- cost of heating, lighting, cleaning and maintenance, and so on;

- rent or interest on the capital cost of the building;

- depreciation;

- employment costs of instructors;

- employment costs of ancillary staff;

- cost of stationery, postage and so on;

- travelling and accommodation expenses paid to trainees;

- cost of training devices and materials used during training.

The costs will be reduced if the trainees make a contribution to output. If managers and other staff are involved part-time as instructors then their employment costs must be suitably apportioned.

Where training is being done at or on-the-job, the trainee is not only using resources but may be causing a loss of profit by preventing those resources from being used effectively in normal production. It is usually difficult to predict the extent of cost in such cases and they must be assessed by making either spot checks or continuous analysis of:

- increases in material wasted;

- losses of production;

- time spent by staff on training in departments where trainees are working.

If the organisation employs a training specialist then these employment costs and those of ancillary staff must be considered.

Value of Costing

Each organisation must decide for itself the value of collecting any but the most obvious costs of training. Where the problem is of apportioning costs, a continuous assessment may be far too expensive and occasional spot checks will give a sufficient guide. Elaborate costing is worth doing only when some use will be made of the results. The main uses of costing will be for control and for making decisions about future training activities. Control of expenditure can be achieved only by:

- knowing its cause – the decision that led to the outlay of cash;

- determining its nature in terms of its continuity, its response to action and its effects on other factors of cost in the business.

Current decisions about training may be committing capital and current expenditure in the future. Realistically, any value to be obtained should be compared with the cost on some basis which relates present values to expenditure, taking account of the time elapsed, for example the discounted cash flow method. However, it is unlikely that the accuracy of the estimating required to determine cost, or to evaluate benefit to be derived, would justify this costing refinement.

13

Costing Treatment of Training Costs

Basically, it would be desirable to find a total cost of training in every case in order to be able to measure the effects of training decisions made by managers. It would be equally valuable to know total training costs for each category of staff so that they can be included in the cost of turnover. However, it is important to recognise that costing itself involves cost and time.

The purpose of collecting and analysing costs is to:

- enable managers and supervisors to control expenditure consequent upon their decisions;

- offer a guide to the magnitude of the problem, thus indicating how much effort is justified to ensure the best value for its money;

- afford a basis for comparison of cost incurred in training with the other opportunities which could be seized if the expenditure on training was transferred to them.

Each organisation has to decide on the costing method best suited to its size, technology and structure. There is little point in a small business installing a complex system for recording training costs, apportioning policy expenditure and isolating total training costs if its needs are limited to the training of five to ten people each year. On the other hand, in a large operation, particularly one in which the management is wholly committed to the view that training is profitable, it may be worth organising the costing of training to a high degree to ensure that this expenditure is as closely and carefully examined as any other activity in the business.

Wherever possible, the documentation that is needed for the business operation should be designed to throw up training costs automatically, for example time sheet and wage analysis abstracts. Unless the cost of training is a very large part of the total operating costs it is unlikely to be profitable to create new documentation to record training costs. Existing records can usually be fairly simply adapted to meet the real needs.

Methods of Costing

CONTINUOUS COLLECTION AND ANALYSIS

This would form part of the cost accounting and budgeting system of the business, requiring forecasts from the manager of numbers to be trained each year. It would also form part of the cost reporting procedure and would be subjected to the whole range of cost control procedures – standard costs, variance reporting, activity forecasting and flexible adjustment control.

SINGLE CALCULATIONS FOR EACH CATEGORY OF EMPLOYEE

The amount would be charged to a department whenever it employed new staff. This project cost would need to be adjusted with changes in rates of pay and other costs and would need revision whenever a new method of training was introduced. Such an approach might be used to report to managers the effect of their operation, particularly the cost of turnover or the extra staff required to implement their decision on new products, new methods or changes in staffing.

SAMPLING PROCEDURES

These can provide an estimate of the relation between training costs and total costs for a particular type of expenditure. For instance, it has been calculated that, in a medium-sized engineering business, the costs of salaries and related items incurred in effective training are about 4 per cent of the total annual salaries bill. This compares with the overall investment percentages already quoted. Such estimates may have little value as a control mechanism, but may be useful in other ways such as estimating and forecasting expenditure.

Costing of Time

For purposes of cost analysis, the methods of training termed 'off-the-job,' 'at-the-job' and 'on-the-job' have different characteristics. Periods of training off-the-job are easily recognisable and, if of significant duration, can be recorded. Such training will result in the acquisition of basic skill and knowledge, but is unlikely to contribute anything of value in terms of saleable product or other profit to the firm. It has therefore the appearance of incurring cost without return. The same is true of the at-the-job or supernumerary type of training, where the trainee is extra to normal staffing.

It is at the on-the-job stage of training that there is the first evidence of return to the organisation in terms of the value gained for the training costs incurred. Learning on-the-job is much quicker in many cases and achieves much higher ultimate efficiency if the requisite investment in off-the-job and at-the-job has been made.

The diagram in Figure 13.1 shows a quite normal relationship between learning time and ultimate production acquired:

Figure 13.1   Output from on-the-job and off-the-job training

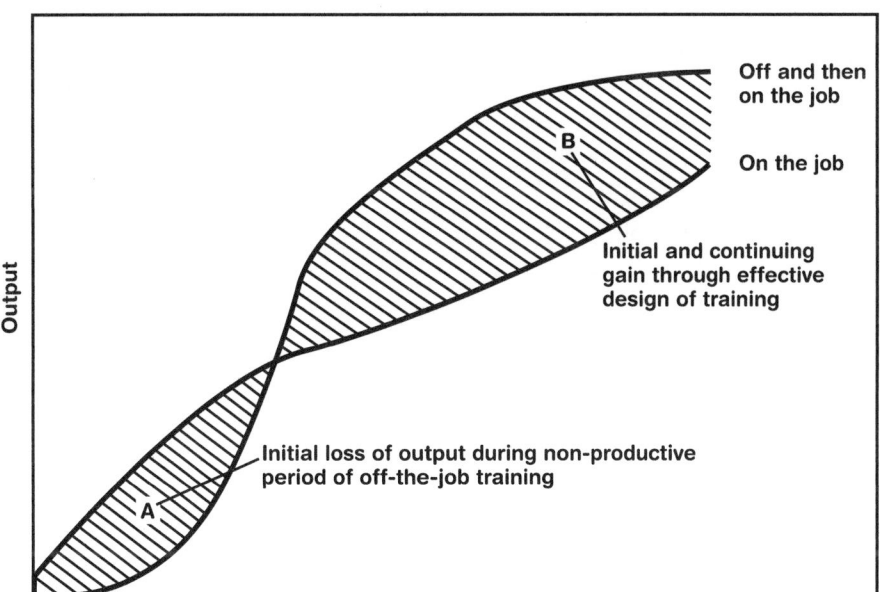

- with on-the-job training only;

- with on-the-job training preceded by effective development of skill and knowledge off-the-job.

Area *A* indicates the initial loss of output caused by the non-productive period off-the-job training. The amount of loss depends largely on the complexity of the learning to be acquired.

Area *B* indicates the continuing gain from effectively designed training.

Where the average length of employment is short and the learning very simple indeed then *A* is likely to exceed *B* and there is no case for any extended period of costly off-the-job training. In most cases, however, it is clear that *B* will greatly exceed *A* and the cost of training will be thus much reduced. However, such an approach does mean taking the decision to train for some time before any contribution can be seen – with the associated problem that training costs will be shown in reports on expenditure before their effect is seen.

Cost Centres and Cost Units

The items of training costs will vary from organisation to organisation but in any case training costs may be related to training activity in two ways: to cost centres or to cost units. In order to carry out training and produce the trained 'cost unit' it is necessary to establish departments to perform the following functions:

- establish training needs;

- recruit and select staff;

- design courses;

- arrange courses – recruit and select trainees, organise course material, aids and so on, train instructors;

- run courses – direct courses and instructors and the use of training aids, arrange examinations and inspections;

- service courses – provide aids and administration;

- assess training – validation and evaluation;

- manage the training function;

- provide general services.

In a small training establishment one person or a small group may carry out all of these jobs. In a large organisation each function may justify a separate staff and supervisor. Each function or combination of them could therefore constitute a training cost centre. The manager of each section will be responsible for the costs incurred in that section.

A controversial item in the list is recruitment and selection of staff which would include advertising, visits to schools and universities by senior staff, making prestige films and so forth. These items are justified since they may help to reduce wastage during training and labour turnover thereafter. It would be short-sighted to exclude these costs since economy in these directions may ultimately involve much higher overall costs.

The cost of training may be established in the first place on a functional or cost basis because this is most convenient for the purposes of budgetary control. The output of the training process is the trained individual and it may be useful to know the unit cost of providing opportunities for learning. This will be built up from the direct costs of the trainee, such as wages or salary, plus the indirect costs arising from the use of the cost centres. Establishing the unit cost will involve apportionment and allocation and there must be a comprehensive list of the costs likely to be incurred. A typical list is given in the Appendix to this chapter.

There is no generally accepted classification of training 'cost units' beyond the vague distinctions between skilled, semi-skilled and unskilled work. The following categories might, however, be used:

- operative;

- craft;

- technician;

- commercial;

- graduate trainee;

- supervisory;

- management;

- others (perhaps bringing out scientists and design and development specialists separate categories).

The commercial group covers administrative, clerical and office staff. Supervisory grades may include foremen and the management category may include works supervisor and department managers. 'Other workers' may include catering staff.

Other categories may be based on the function within which an individual works, for example sales, human resources, transport and so on.

Training is often identified by the type of qualification obtained. It can also be sub-divided into initial, refresher and retraining. It is often classified according to whether it is full- or part-time, day or evening, sandwich or block release, residential or non-residential, and so on. The categories generally do not seem to have an objective basis since they differ markedly from one area to another.

Confusion arises between occupational classification and the classification of trainees; these are not synonymous. An apprentice will only be a trainee undergoing training whether this be on- or off-the-job.

ESTABLISHING THE NUMBER OF TRAINEES

The correct measure to take is the number of trainees completing the course. Where training extends over more than one year, the number still in training at the end of each year may be taken.

Comparison may be facilitated by expressing these units in terms of trainee-years. One trainee taking a one-year course is the equivalent of 13 trainees taking a four-week course. These units may also be used in apportioning general training overhead to each category of training.

Standard Costing Method

Figure 13.2 is an example of the way in which costs of training can be collected and analysed. Expenditure on training is analysed for each grade of apprentice defined as:

- *Craft:* serving an apprenticeship with day release.

- *Technician:* normally working for higher qualification on a day release basis, for example drawing office apprentices.

- *Technologist (student):* four- or five-years training organised on a full-time basis and leading to a professional qualification.

- *Graduate:* a two-year course of practical training following a degree, or divided into one year before and one year after university.

- *Commercial:* commercial trainees who are granted day release.

The analysis does not include the costs involved when a trainee is working alongside a skilled person since it is usually impossible to identify them. It also does not include credit items like prestige, reduction of labour turnover and increased efficiency which are also more difficult to accurately cost.

The cost of training may be an allowable expense for tax purposes.

Appendix 13a: Examples of Costs Relating to Training

PEOPLE COSTS AND PAYMENTS

Account

100   Salaries – ordinary time

101   Salaries – overtime

102   Wages – casual and part-time

103   Commission

104   Bonuses

Figure 13.2   A standard method of costing the training of apprentices

DESCRIPTION	EXPENDITURE PER GRADE OF APPRENTICE/TRAINEE					Total Expenditure
	Craft	Technician	Technologist	Graduate	Commercial	
	£	£	£	£	£	£

1 Wages and salaries (taxable)
    Apprentices – for time spent in works and offices and at college or courses
    Instructors – Full-time or part-time
    Clerical and Administrative – to include allocation of training and/or HR department effort
    Statutory and Social – Payment for statutory and annual holidays, National Insurance, and company contribution to pension scheme
  Total cost for wages and salaries						

2 Maintenance of training centre or defined training area
    Rents
    Rates and taxes
    Depreciation of fixed assets (plant, buildings, etc.)
    Light fuel and power
    Indirect manpower costs
    Maintenance of machine tools
    Maintenance of other equipment of a capital nature
    (Shop tools, fixtures, equipment and materials, etc.)
    Consumable equipment
    (Training material, stationery, etc.)
  Total cost of training centre or area						

3 Recruitment and selection Advertising of vacancies, apprenticeship brochure, school visits, selection processes (including cost of interviewing, testing, entertainment, etc.) travelling expenses (of candidates and staff)						

4 Fees
    Fees paid to colleges etc.
    Cost of external courses and educational visits
  Total cost of fees						

5 Awards Books, tools or prizes, cost of prize-giving ceremony – parents' day, etc.						

Figure 13.2   Continued

DESCRIPTION	EXPENDITURE PER GRADE OF APPRENTICE/TRAINEE					Total Expenditure
	Craft	Technician	Technologist	Graduate	Commercial	
	£	£	£	£	£	£
6 Fringe benefits Meals, subsidised travel, apprentice association, sports and recreational activities, etc.						
7 Accommodation Cost of lodging allowances, provision of hostels, etc.						
8 Donations and subscriptions To external bodies for training purposes						
9 Any other items Please detail GROSS COSTS CREDIT ITEMS (i.e. Valuation of apprentices' production if done by skilled people) NET COSTS (i.e. Gross costs less credit items) UNIT COSTS i.e. ____(net costs)____ (number of apprentices)						

Note: * This should include any relevant payments for overtime or bonus.

PEOPLE COSTS, OTHER PAYMENTS

Account

110   National Insurance

111   Luncheon vouchers and gross cost of meals

112   Pension fund contributions

113   Fees to consultants, auditors, counsel, and so on

114   Accommodation (hotels and hostels)

115   Miscellaneous

FEES PAID FOR EXTERNAL TRAINING

Account

120   Fees paid for training courses

121   Fees paid to research establishments

122   Fees paid to consultants

123   Fees to local authorities

124   Fees to universities and other non-profit-making institutions

BUILDING COSTS AND SERVICES

Account

130   Rent

131   Rates

132   Water

133   Repairs and maintenance

134   Security

135   Fire prevention

136   Electricity

137   Gas

138   Oil

PRODUCTION COSTS

Account

140   Machine hire and rental

141   Outwork and sub-contractors

142   Royalties

143   Machine repairs and maintenance

ADMINISTRATION COSTS

Account

150   Printing and stationery

151   Postages and packaging

152   Telephone, computer and so on

153   Newspapers and periodicals

154   Subscriptions

155   Furniture, office machine repairs and maintenance

156   Meetings and excursions

INSURANCES

Account

160   Employers' liability

161   Accident

162   Fire

163   Burglary

164   Fidelity bond

165   Cash in transit

166   Vehicle

TRANSPORTATION AND TRAVEL

Account

170   Vehicle licences

171   Vehicle repairs and maintenance

172   Petrol and oil

173   Travel expenses and fares

DEPRECIATION AND OTHER PROVISIONS

Account

180   Land and buildings

181   Plant and machinery

182   Vehicles

183   Furniture and office machines

184   Patents and trade-marks

PURCHASING AND SELLING EXPENSES

Account

190   Advertising for products and staff

191   Commission other than staff

192   Carriage inwards

193   Custom duties

194   Carriage outwards

ADJUSTMENT OR RECIPROCAL ACCOUNTS

Materials – Account

210   Production materials used at actual cost

211   Production materials used at standard cost

212   Loose tools

This list will be modified in the light of the requirements of each business. It is a subjective list of expenses and in order to establish the cost of training it is necessary to allocate the items in relation to their objective. Those costs which relate to training must be separated from those which do not and then be associated with training activities.

14

Planning for Training and Controlling Training Costs

Wherever and whenever cost is generated by management by making a decision, unnecessary cost will arise unless careful and constant control is exercised. This is as true of training costs as of any other.

At the same time, for training as for any other sphere of business, it is quite clear that unless definite objectives have been set and plans laid for effective operation to achieve those objectives, the costs of operation will be excessive, will grow needlessly and will result in much reduced added value to the business or service.

It follows that one major objective of planning the training function is to set budgets for costs and this presupposes that:

- As with any major feature of the business, the training activity has been planned and that adequate training forecasts have been made upon the basis of a training needs analysis – as described earlier.

- Training expenses to achieve the plans have been identified to the degree that management has deemed necessary.

- Expenses have been classified according to cause and characteristics.

- The responsibility for the expenditure has been established.

- There is the facility available to record, control and feed back to the training decision makers the actual results of their decisions as compared with the expected results, and the predicted expenditure needed to achieve the result required.

Any business activity must be planned if the business is to avoid the evil consequences of management by crisis. This does not mean that business plans must always be set down in a particular or complex form. It means simply that someone should have thought ahead sufficiently to avoid unnecessary cost and achieve the optimum state in relation to the business objectives.

In the training field there are, and should be, considerable differences in the way training plans are made and implemented. The manager of the smallest business, having done planning, may easily memorise details, do calculations on the back of an envelope, give directions simply by talking with subordinates, and be extremely effective. In businesses of size, responsibility must be delegated and, with any delegation of authority over staff, there will be a corresponding responsibility for the training and development of that staff.

In these circumstances there is certain to be a need to formalise the planning, budgeting and control techniques. Such formalisation requires that plans and procedures be committed to paper and agreed so that all concerned can work together.

Planning

The training plan is based on time, taking a projection of anticipated activity and expressing the expected costs and outcome in measurable terms. Money is the usual unit used, since it is the ultimate financial outcome which is seen as important.

It may, however, be sufficient to express a plan in other terms, for example, number of student weeks, or percentage of total working time spent on training.

Several items of anticipated training expenditure will vary with the circumstances arising and for such items a flexible plan should be created – for example, if the number of recruits is doubled then the anticipated direct cost of training, which is proportional for the number of trainees, will need to be doubled correspondingly. A change in technique of training due to a large increase or decrease in the retraining of staff must be capable of being reflected in the plan.

Operational Control

Operational control is achieved by periodic comparison of the plan with the actual results achieved and objective analysis of the causes of any differences found, the positive or negative variances.

These two processes are embraced in the technique of budgetary control, and the process of budgeting for training should take its place in the overall budgeting of the organisation's activities along with others subsidiary to the master budget.

The purpose of budgetary control is to direct the attention of management to the divergences between plan and operation so that action can be taken to correct the situation while there is time to revise the plan to more realistic objectives.

This means that the responsibility of any item of expense must be allocated to one person, the manager or supervisor who has the authority to make those decisions that affect the result. No one should be held responsible for something that they cannot directly control. The budget centres to which expenditure will be charged must coincide with the organisational structure of management.

In the training field this obvious rule creates some difficulty. It is plainly the responsibility of the line and department managers to make the decisions about the training of their staff but, in most cases, they are likely to turn to a training specialist, possibly running a training centre and in charge of a number of training resources. The ultimate efficiency of the training is thus affected by two people each contributing to the result.

Taking the cost of payments to trainees whilst undergoing training at a training centre, it would seem sensible to make the training specialist in charge of the centre responsible for this cost in some way. This would give the incentive to shorten the time required for the trainee to learn to the required standard.

The logical conclusion is that in the training field there are areas of cost which are the joint responsibility of the line departmental manager and the training specialist.

Special Project Planning

Special project planning or analysis is used when a specific project is proposed and it would be useful to forecast how future income and expenditure will be affected over the project's life.

For instance, a business introducing a scheme of rewards related to a productivity agreement may propose to train the managers and supervisors, office staff, specialist staff, craftsmen, operators and shop stewards in the procedures to be carried out in the future, the reallocation of duties and the means of measurement. This training project, which concerns the business as a whole, may be the subject of a special project budget of expenditure which could be separately recorded and controlled from day to day.

Assuming that a project budget has been created for this training, the training specialist in charge should be required to administer the programme in accordance with it.

Standard budget periods are usually laid down in an organisation. The training budget must conform with the company's financial structure which may call for yearly forecasts, quarterly adjustments to forecast and monthly reporting of differences.

Types of Budget

There are basically two types of budget for training activity:

1. For the training done within departments and for which the line or departmental managers are responsible directly. For example, if there is an apprentice training school within the engineering section and the instructors report to the engineering section manager, they are responsible for this expenditure. It ought therefore to be included in the budget and controlled.

2. For the training costs incurred in planning for training, administering it and providing specific training where necessary is the responsibility of the training manager.

The costs which the training manager can directly control should form part of the budget for the training department or function of the business.

The training manager's budget should deal with those items directly controlled. It should provide sufficient flexibility to give a means of control appropriate to the fluctuating demands on his activity.

Training is not yet a science in which the results of action can be accurately predicted and the approach to budgeting for training should acknowledge this fact and be so structured as to allow for both the known and the unknown factors in the activities of the department.

In a well-established business the trainer should, by consulting with others, be able to predict reasonably accurately the number of trainees who will be undertaking on any particular courses or programmes of training. However, it may not be possible to predict changes in training need caused by some change in the environment over which there is no control.

For instance, a business using salesmen to sell a popular consumer durable product may decide to move to a planned presentation type of selling approach, thus necessitating a completely new type of training for new salesmen and the advent of a need for retraining the established salesmen. The budget should be capable of adjustment at intervals to take account of such change and the consequent increased or decreased training expenditure in terms of the preparation of new training material, new visual aids, time spent in briefing the lecturers and contributors to a new type of course, length of the course and degree of proficiency on leaving the training centre. In such cases it may well be that, because of a greater formalisation of the selling procedure, less time will be required for training in a training centre off-the-job, but this can be supplemented by e-learning.

As with most budgets, the training budget will usually be based on past records, and the process is one of estimating the change from a previous budget. An accurate forecast of expense can only be made if there are records (relating cause and effect) from previous years to support decisions for the coming period. Starting from scratch it will probably take three or four years of budget experiments before a truly realistic training budget can be expected.

Fixed Costs

Which are fixed costs, what causes these to rise or fall and what is the time cycle of decisions in relation to each?

If it is assumed that the following are the fixed costs of a training centre:

- salaries of training staff;

- salaries of support staff;

- rent and rates of space occupied;

- utilities such as heat, light, water, telephones;

- stationery and supplies;

- cleaning and maintenance.

Then it is possible to discover how each of these is affected.

Taking training staff as an instance, the following information is required:

- What numbers of training staff are needed at any level of activity?

- What level of activity is predicted for the training centre over the next four or five years?

- What is the least time required before a new member of the training staff is competent?

- Is the aim to have training staff highly specialised in particular areas of training or will they be trained to cover a wide field?

- What are the salary ranges for the training staff, at what point will such staff be recruited from outside or within, what sort of percentage increase in such salaries is expected either from a movement upwards of the salary range due to cost of living or market forces, or due to merit increases?

Such a cost is probably represented by a curve showing increases stepped with activity and a steady overall increase.

Thus there is no such thing as a permanently fixed cost. The term is used to distinguish persistent costs, arising from overall decisions about the provision of human and material resources, from the variable costs such as:

- Training material – books, computers, handouts, material and training aids.

- Travelling expenses and subsistence which tend to vary directly with short-term changes in activity.

Figure 14.1   Increases in fixed costs

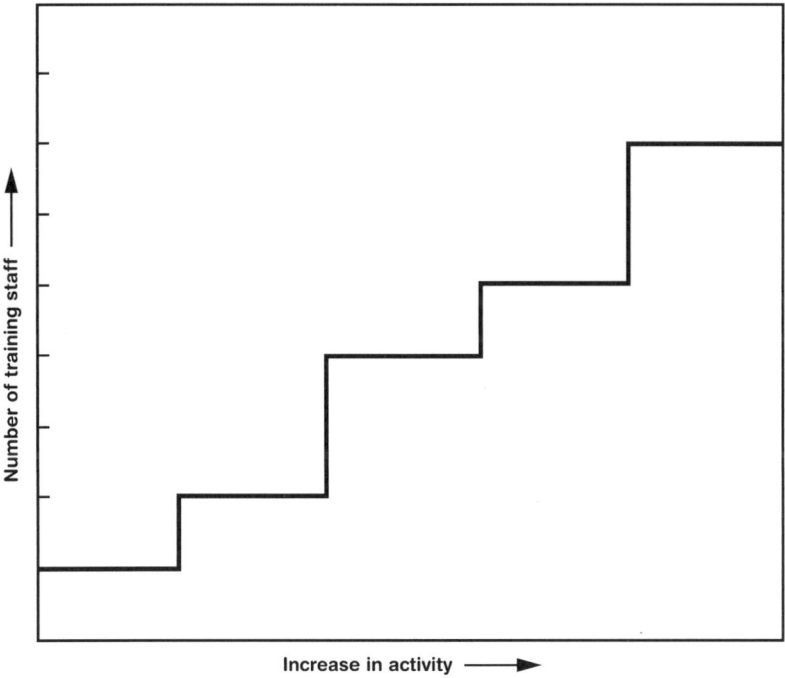

Basic Decisions

When setting up a budget for training, some basic decisions have to be taken which correspond to those made when a budget for any service department is established:

- What methods does the accounting department use; how do they classify expenditure; will there need to be amendments or additions to the current classification?

- What training records will be kept and how will they be used: will they be integrated into the business data processing operation or will they be kept separately?

- What is the attitude to charging between departments; if senior managers take part in a seminar will their salaries, travelling and other expenses be charged to the training department?

- Will trainees be supplied with computers, text books, training manuals and other materials?

Such questions – and the questions they are bound to generate – will provide the basis for the training budget, leading to specific answers where these were previously unpredictable but unavoidable unknown factors in the training situation.

Indirect Costs in Budgets

Any budget will account for the direct costs that apply only to the training operation but there are good arguments both for excluding indirect costs and for including them. On the one hand, the training manager should not waste time seeking to explain changes in cost controlled elsewhere, for example an increase in VAT or insurance premiums. Yet, if the business is to be profitable, every manager must be kept aware of the cost of the resources used and of the services provided to support the activity.

For any business it is a technical costing question how this dilemma is to be solved. In general it appears that a marginal costing approach, where each individual is made responsible for the costs directly controlled, gives the greatest incentives to individual managers to operate with cost effectiveness.

If this view is adopted it is essential that at intervals the managers concerned should be given some measure of the trend of costs in providing resources and support to them. Periodic studies of potential cost reduction should support any cost control procedures.

Certainly when project planning, for example estimating the total costs of mounting a special series of courses, all the costs incurred must somehow be brought into consideration. If it is possible to establish the ratio of allocatable costs to directly controlled costs by a special study, then a percentage can be added to the estimated direct costs of a training project. This will give an approximation to total cost which is probably sufficiently accurate in view of the difficulties of evaluation of training.

Accounting Treatment of Training Costs

The costs of training have to be incorporated in the costing system so that they are absorbed in the total cost of producing and selling. There are three possible approaches to this problem.

DISTRIBUTION OF COSTS

Each department accepts a charge from the training department. The total of these charges is equal to the total allocated cost of the training department. The basis on which operating departments are asked to contribute might be any one of a number – the numbers employed, turnover, output, and so on.

The danger with such a method is that it does not relate to actual use of the services of the training department, nor does it give any incentive to the training manager to reduce cost since all costs will be charged out from that department in any case.

SELLING THE SERVICE

The training department sells its services at fixed rates to the consumer departments, the aim being to cover the allocated costs. This method has the advantage that managers called upon to pay for the training done for their staff will test the price against the advantage gained realistically and this will act as an automatic check on the value of the training – from the manager's point of view.

The problem that this method creates is that there may be fluctuations of demand on the training department due to market conditions, economic changes and the like which are spasmodic and temporary. Fluctuations in demand of this kind on the training department may prevent the training department from building up an effective staff over a long period and equipping itself with resources matching the required developments now being made in training technology.

POLICY COSTS

Certain training costs are regarded as company policy costs and stated as such in the accounts. They are accumulated and shown as a deduction from the gross profit of the business in the same way as for any other policy cost. The whole directly controllable training cost may be treated in this way. From the accounting point of view, it is the simplest approach, but it does mean that control over the expenditure is likely to be less rigorous than it should be.

Where a business operates a training programme which is designed to ensure overall effective manpower availability irrespective of particular departmental needs – as in a management training development scheme or a commercial apprenticeship scheme – this approach may be viable. It does, however, mean that the objectives should be very clearly stated and the results reviewed frequently and objectively.

Controlling Costs

Having established the costs for which the training manager is responsible, how each of these costs is caused, and what factors create change in them, the control mechanism is relatively easy for any competent accountant to achieve. A simple columnar worksheet does the job quite effectively:

BUDGET

- class of expense – code;

- description of item;

- section – supervisor or manager responsible;

- amount budgeted for period;

- basis of budget amount;

- actual activity for period;

- activity difference – initial budget versus adjusted budget;

- adjusted budget for period.

ACTUAL

- expense incurred;

- offsetting income;

- difference – adjusted budget versus expense;

- causes of difference;

- alternative courses of action;

- to consolidate benefit gained;

- to eliminate losses incurred;

- need for revision of budget.

The last item is most important for future operations. A formal method of amending budgets is essential to create the conditions for discussion between managers who have the need of training their staff and the training manager who assists them to fulfil this need.

15

Evaluation of Training

It is not possible to measure accurately the value of training except by creating a completely artificial situation where the other variables are held constant and the training is either:

- introduced where none existed before;

- eliminated if apparently successful methods and learning exist;

- varied in method in some specifically prescribed fashion.

To say this is not to make the training activity any more difficult to decide about than many other activities in business today. The same statement can be made about research and development, pension funds, social clubs, sickness payment, fringe benefits to staff, working conditions, public relations activity, productivity agreements and many others.

However, it is quite clear that there is a growth of attention to the subject of training and an increased cost incurred for the training of people to high levels of technical competence. This has meant a recognition that we can no longer afford to think of training in the 'faith, hope and charity' way of past. Training, if it is to be accepted as an essential integral part of the business, must stand up to rigorous investigation of its worth – even if at times this can only be done by dint of persistent questioning.

What is Evaluation?

Evaluation is the process of putting a value on the benefits stemming from the training process in social as well as financial terms.

The purpose of evaluation is to determine whether or not the objectives and content of training activities are consistent with the current needs of the organisation, if the objectives are being reached in the most effective and economical way and, if not, what changes should be made. Successful evaluation of training, in the final analysis, must be the result of an assessment and comparison of employee competence before and after training. Evaluation at each step in planning and implementing training programmes is necessary, however, in order to make timely adjustments to programmes and approaches.

The term 'evaluation' should not be confused with the term 'validation'. Validation is a process carried out to see that the training given has been successful in achieving its aim. This aim may have been based on an erroneous view of the learning need but the training may have been successful in terms of the objectives set.

The connecting link between validation and evaluation is, of course, the checking of the stated aims of the training process to ascertain whether they were based on real learning needs. Reference is sometimes made to 'external validation,' that is, deciding whether the aims were the right ones to go for, and 'internal validation,' that is, did the training result in the learner learning what it was intended. Is performance in line with the stated objectives in terms of applied skill and knowledge?

At the end of this chapter there is an attempt to demonstrate by a questioning technique – value analysis type – how widespread are the benefits to be obtained from the application of effective training. Meanwhile it is important to understand what must be evaluated if the purposes of evaluation are to be achieved.

In general terms, comprehensive evaluation should include assessment of:

- The validity of the training policy and the plan to apply this policy to the discovered learning need.

- The way in which learners are given opportunities to learn and are motivated to learn – in other words the training and instruction methods, materials, aids, location and ability of people giving the training.

- The ultimate results in terms of the performance, achievement or changed behaviour of those who have learned.

Assessing Progress

Measurement is the prime difficulty here. The technique frequently adopted is to test the trainee by some form of examination. Written examinations are frequently used but have three disadvantages:

1. They cannot possibly cover the entire syllabus.

2. They are unlikely to be acceptable to mature students.

3. The assessment of written examinations is very unreliable. Different examiners give inconsistent marks to the same examinee and the same examiner can be inconsistent in the marking of different papers.

On the other hand, examinations do provide a motivation to learn which can be effective in areas where the material to be learned is basic to the learning need but is not obviously connected with the expected performance. In the training of technicians, technologists and specialists such as accountants, purchasing officers and human resource staff, examinations on the subject may well be the fundamental testing process. Managers need to have fundamental knowledge of the way in which people behave in response to certain situations and how groups operate. Such knowledge can be tested by examinations of the right kind.

There is a lot of work to be done in redesigning examinations for this purpose, and there are moves afoot in many institutions to replace the essay type of examination with examinations that can be marked objectively, such as those containing the forced choice type of question.

In some areas, particularly those requiring the application of a manual or perceptual skill, an achievement test – milling a piece of material to certain limits, or information feeding into a computer – can be used to measure the reasonable accuracy. The problem here is whether the test shall be limited in time and assessment made on the performance during that time, taking into account the errors made, or whether time should be allowed for the learner to complete the test to the specification demanded and the assessment based on the time required to achieve this.

- *Collecting opinions.* In many cases, particularly in management training, assessment is performed by collecting a number of opinions.

- *Comments from trainees.* By question and comment during the last session of a course. This is not very satisfactory, being too close to the experience to judge objectively. These comments can be collected by 'stock-taking groups' (small, informal discussion groups) who present corporate assessments or by written questionnaire sent two or three weeks after the course.

- *Comments for instructors.* An experienced trainer, speaker or course organiser can usually judge whether the course is going well and meeting its objectives and the needs of trainees.

- *Comments from management.* Assuming management has been consulted about the content of the programme or level of staff for whom intended, comments from managers after discussion with their own trainees will indicate the extent to which objectives have been met.

The collection of opinions to test the effectiveness of a training operation such as a management training course can be very useful if done properly, but the opinions of the managers or supervisors who are to control the training in the future must be included. In other words, there must be complete participation by all concerned.

One effective addition to the opinion-collecting method of evaluation is the appointment of a mentor for each trainee to whom one can go in confidence to discuss the application of their learning to the job in hand. This mentor should be someone who knows the realities of the job to be undertaken, probably having done it, and is able to iron out any difficulties that the learner has in seeing the application of what has been learned to the task to be done. Such mentors can feed back to the organisers of the training the very real problems which trainees find in transferring knowledge gained in an off-the-job or an at-the-job supernumerary situation to the reality of doing the job.

Assessment after Training

The level and quality of the job performance over a period of time following the training must be assessed, and this can be done only by applying those measures of performance that are pertinent to the job as it is normally performed. It is fundamental to such assessment that data about the performance is collected periodically and is related to time to give a learning curve for each trainee. The shape of this learning curve will indicate the trainee's rate of progress and highlight any needs for further training to overcome particular misunderstanding or slow development of skill.

Trainee's Targets

When is a trainee trained? It is essential that a trainee should be given targets of performance at which to aim both during the learning process and during the practice on-the-job. The actual performance compared with these targets should be fed back to the trainee to see development over the period and thus gain the satisfaction of demonstrating ability. These targets need careful design in order that they shall be neither too difficult nor too easy to achieve, because in either case there will be a reduced motivation to learn.

Calculating the Benefits of Training

In some areas it is possible to make calculations of the benefits given by training. These cases are those where the output of the trainee can be measured directly. For example, it is easily possible to measure the learning time of an operative working alone on an article, the quality of which can be assessed. Gilding in the pottery industry is a good illustration of such a task. In this case comparison can be made between the time taken to learn by one training method and the time taken by a different method. The quality can be assessed and the rate of output measured in terms of units of crockery gilded. Another example is selling direct to retailers where it is possible to measure the number of calls made, the amount of goods sold, the returns from customers due to overstocking, the number of customers ceasing to trade with the company, and the number of new customers created.

Even in the case of sales, measurement may be necessary over a long period, since the selling approach made by the individual may be extremely successful in the short term but, by its very nature, may be creating long-term problems for the business. Unfortunately, apart from such tasks, the output of which can be measured directly, placing a value on training in order to achieve a cost/benefit analysis of the process is extremely difficult. Measurement is the heart of the difficulty, plus the problem of predicting how current behaviour will affect future operations.

The advent of the techniques of setting measurable objectives for managers will, when it is operative, give a measure of the effectiveness of training but even when this is done it will still be extremely difficult to put a money value on many of the objectives that are set. Certainly as many objectives as possible should be set in quantifiable terms so that they serve as effective controls.

In any situation evidence can be accumulated about the effect of training, but in a vast number of cases these effects cannot be quantified financially. Advanced thinking in the field of training recognises that the evaluation of training is even more complex than has been considered to date.

There is the artificial distinction that is made first between skill and knowledge and later between knowledge and attitude. For the convenience of designing training programmes these distinctions appear to be useful. This utility may be illusory since each of these is part of the other two, and is completely dependent upon the existence of the others. This being so, it is possible that by insisting on the division for programme purposes, difficulties may be created which need not exist.

It is quite clear that learning is a continuous process of change and is related to other processes of change for example, age with its mental and physical effects. It could be that, if we are to maintain training as a profitable contribution to the business, we must observe and influence continuously the individual changes and the organisational changes which are happening. This makes training – creating opportunity to learn – a completely continuous process even in one job. It follows that the role of every supervisor and manager in any business is very largely a training role and should be seen as such. The aim is the creation of a learning organisation.

Training is a process going on for people designed for a purpose and influenced by everything that is done by it, to it, or for it. It has therefore to be seen that any attempts to measure a factor in the system will, of itself, be an influence on the system which will have effect. Thus, before deciding on any complex measure of the effects of training on individuals or groups in the system – for example, by questionnaire designed to ascertain pre-training and post-training attitudes – the question must be posed as to the effect of the questionnaire itself on the attitude to be changed.

Case Histories

Some case histories of the benefit of training in textiles are:

NARROW FABRICS BUSINESS (105 EMPLOYEES)

The basic training of weavers used to take six weeks. Since the training instructors attended a course on Systematic Operative Training trainee weavers achieve the same efficiency in two or three weeks.

YARN PROCESSING BUSINESS (260 EMPLOYEES)

Since selected experienced operatives attended a training instructors' course, they have prepared job breakdowns for ten occupations and have developed a comprehensive induction programme for new entrants. In some occupations, the training time for new entrants has been reduced by 50 per cent. In all cases, the reductions exceed 30 per cent.

YARN DYEING BUSINESS (40 EMPLOYEES)

The instructor in this case was a director of the company who had attended a course for trainers. It took ten days to prepare the training programme, after which the training time for one job was reduced from six months to four weeks. In other areas, the results were not quite as dramatic, but well worthwhile. For one of the processes, the training now takes ten days instead of 24, to achieve the same efficiency. At another process, trainees have completed their basic training in ten days compared with 40 days.

ZIP FASTENER BUSINESS (55 EMPLOYEES)

Systematic training by qualified training instructors has reduced training times by 50 per cent.

DYEING BUSINESS (65 EMPLOYEES)

When this company engaged its first new entrant as a dyeing operative, following attendance by its training instructor at a course organised in conjunction with a group training scheme, it was astonished by the results.

After one-day's instruction, the trainee equalled previous trainees' progress after five days. After four days, progress was equal to four weeks under the previous system, and the quality of work was better than from any existing operative. The firm was convinced that this was due to the development of a training programme which was written after the instructor's analysis of the job. More instructors will now be trained on approved courses for work in other departments.

On the face of it there would seem to be complete justification for the introduction of these particular training methods. It is extremely unlikely that their cost will exceed the value obtained from the results, but it is possible.

In a number of books on training, in particular *Industrial Skills and Industrial Training for Manual Operations* by David W. Douglas Seymour and *Training within the Organisation* by David King, a number of calculations are shown which are of the same order as the illustrations above. Douglas Seymour did in his books attempt to do a cost/benefit analysis for a number of jobs where skills analysis has been applied. These analyses, however, are confined to comparison of production and costs and are not measured against the costs of the training given. However, the process of cost/benefit analysis in training is one which needs much more study.

Essentially, two processes are important: (1) wherever possible measuring the learning time before and after the introduction of a particular training method or change in method, together with the change in ultimate efficiency; and (2) from this a judgement is necessary as to whether the training process has been worthwhile. In many cases, particularly where no training has been done, or very primitive training has been done, the evidence will be overwhelming without financial measurement.

However, there will be many cases where either such measurements are not available, or the improvements shown in reduction of learning time and efficiency are not of themselves convincing reasons for the introduction of new training methods or a change in method. In such cases it is only possible to rely upon a value analysis approach which questions frequently the validity of the reasoning behind any particular training activity.

Value Analysis Applied to Training

Broadly defined, value analysis is an organised approach designed to identify a real business need and to achieve this at the lowest cost consistent with the maintenance of the *necessary* quality, performance and reliability.

The important word in this definition is 'necessary' and much of the value analysis approach is directed at discovering what is necessary. This may lead to a conclusion that higher quality, performance or reliability are required *or* as is very often the case that lower quality, performance or reliability would suffice for the business as compared with the prevailing current levels. In other words, value analysis can be seen as an organised procedure for the effective identification of unnecessary cost.

The philosophy behind the approach is based on four principles:

1. What is being done now can be improved upon.

2. To recognise the factors in a problem and to challenge any assumptions made to justify the present method of solving that problem is to begin to find a better solution.

3. Average people working together with a common aim will accomplish better than average results.

4. The questioning technique, if kept strictly neutral, will stimulate new thinking in an area which can lead to innovation and change that is profitable to the business.

This philosophy can be applied to the training process with the prospect of real results, but only if there is planning, motivation and positive leadership.

The Appendices to this chapter give a list of principles to be adopted by value analysis and a list of the sort of questions they will ask about training.

Obviously the way in which value analysis of training will be organised depends upon the organisational structure of the firm. The team or group approach has been used frequently and has proved effective in other fields – there is no reason why it should not be equally effective in the training field. Certainly, it is extremely unlikely that any one person could, in a business of any size, be able to implement a value analysis plan on their own. It is suggested that, under a team leader, who should be the top manager whose function is or includes training, there should be a group consisting of a balanced combination of some managers with direct responsibility for training staff, finance and training specialists. This team should meet regularly to review the situation. If there is available, as in some large companies, value analysis specialists the methods to be adopted for making the analysis will be their responsibility.

Appendix 15a: Principles of Value Analysis

- The aim is to improve value and not to protect the prevailing strategies.

- Communication between the members of the group must be effective – exchanging ideas freely, using a high degree of imagination, and stating views as objectively as possible.

- Adequate information must be available. The risk involved in making decisions based on inadequate information has to be weighed against the cost and time taken to acquire all the facts.

- The relationship between the various phases of the inquiry should be recognised. The ultimate plan of training which is to be implemented will be a combination of ideas and a compromise with the ideals of highest performance, complete job satisfaction and lowest learning times.

- Be as objective as possible. Keep remembering the purposes of the team while it is clear that all training must take into account the reactions of people and their sentiments.

- Avoid excess complexity in the study. There is a natural trend towards greater and greater complexity in thinking about an aspect of business such as training which involves the use of economic, psychological and sociological concepts. The simple answer that comes readily to mind is probably as near the truth as is necessary.

Appendix 15b: Questions that Value Analysts will Ask about Training

- What are the specific objectives of the training? How have they been formulated? Are they the result of some form of analysis of what people need to actually do, on-the-job?

- What changes in the individual is the training designed to effect? Is it possible to achieve such changes with these learners? Is it necessary to inculcate new attitudes – a difficult process?

- What are the short-term and long-term benefits that it is thought will be derived if these changes are achieved? Are these benefits measurable? If not, how accurate is the assessment likely to be?

- What organisational inefficiencies will occur if the training is not given? Can these be overcome by some cheaper process?

- What effect will the introduction or development of training have on:

  a. Morale within the organisation?

  b. The image of the organisation to potential recruits?

  c. The image of the organisation within the industry?

- Are these effects important enough to justify the effort required to implement a 'progressive' policy of training?

- What proof is there that the training will improve individual performance? Is someone else doing it differently at less cost? Does the training need all its features? Could it be shortened? Should it be lengthened to achieve significantly greater benefit?

- Could a standard training package be used at less cost than development programmes for individuals? What would be the increase or decrease in quality, performance, and reliability caused by accepting a standard training package?

- Is there available within the business sufficient expertise to answer these questions? If not, how can this be remedied? Are there sufficient training staff and instructors to do the job needed or too many? By what measure shall the strength of the training staff be determined – number per hundred employees – salaries as percentage of payroll – calculation of requirement in terms of trainee weeks – or how?

- What methods of evaluation will be applied to each type of training:

  a. Rsearch with matched groups;

  b. Analysis of some specific results – say rate of accidents as a measure of safety training;

  c. Performance tests on-the-job;

  d. Study of progress records and appraisal reports;

  e. Supervisor's view of effect

  f. Trainee's view of effect;

  g. Pre-training and post-training questionnaires or what?

- Do the methods used take advantage of all that is known of the technology of training, the findings of educational research and the knowledge of the psychology of the learning-teaching process? Are the methods too 'precious' or academic for the type of learner? What investigations should we make to keep up to date?

- Are all the sources of advice about training being utilised – employers' federation, trade associations, COSIRA, consultants, the local college or university, or other specialist advisory bodies?

- Is the firm making any contribution to the development of thinking about training – for the industry, for the locality, for society? Is it part of the objective to do so? Would such research or investigation give the firm an edge over others in terms of efficiency or prestige? If no such contribution is being made what would it cost to do so?

- Is there enough information available about the business to discover those areas where training development might have a beneficial effect? Is the reporting and accounting system designed for rapid information retrieval on which objective judgements can be based?

- Is the training specialist function in the right place in the management organisation structure? Is it too low a level to have sufficient influence? Or, alternatively, is there a gap between the top authority in training matters and the trainers or instructors who actually do the job? Is there sufficient liaison between the managers responsible for training and the people providing the training service? Can any of these be changed to give better value from the training?

16

On-Line Training

Technology Assisted Training

This can be defined as any training designed or delivered with the assistance of technologically-based methods. It is additional to training based on group interaction, conventional instruction and action learning. It helps those new to technology to become familiar with the principles and techniques and the cutting-edge practices in the training field. It does not change the fundamental principles of how people learn. It is a developing art or science and a major target for critical evaluation.

Trainers certainly need to enhance their knowledge and skill related to the new technology. As fewer people are expected to enter long-term training programmes, it becomes vital to look at shorter training inputs over a longer period. More and more of these shorter programmes are needed, particularly as training is recognised as an essential investment, as discussed in previous chapters.

The Concepts

The concepts behind on-line training are not new, although applications have progressed rapidly in the last 10–15 years. There is even some danger that technological ingenuity can outstrip the genuine needs of learners and overcomplicate the training process. 'Classroom' time can be reduced, but only at at massive technological cost in terms of programme preparation, which itself may be quickly outdated.

Analysis of learning needs in the 'on-line' world is based on the same principles as those discussed in Chapter 5. Instructional techniques and principles have not fundamentally changed. The design and achievement of behavioural objectives still reflect the seminal work of Robert F. Mager in *Preparing Instructional Objectives* (Mager, 1997).

Training is sometimes defined as an intervention to meet a number of 'learning domains'. For instance, a machine operator learns to function effectively by some knowledge-based instruction – 'the cognitive domain' – combined with supervised practice – 'the psychomotor domain'. Performance and knowledge can be measured in each domain. Learning can come from information and instructions, supervised practice, information exchange – 'action learning', modelling and so on.

On-line training is primarily concerned with information and instruction. The process is essentially one way although reaction and understanding can be tested. However, recent research has cast doubt on the computer's ability to evaluate creative responses which have not been programmed in.

The on-line/technology contribution to training can be an important and economic means of preparing for action training inside or outside the training room. 'Classroom' training is almost a contradiction in terms, a throwback to memories of old-fashioned 'schooling'. Alas some 'trainers' use PowerPoint to provide this in electronic form!

Experienced trainers, on the other hand, make use of a very wide range of training vehicles: audio visuals, brainstorming, business games, case studies, blackboards, flipcharts, whiteboards, demonstrations, discussions, lectures (as a last resort), modelling, music, panels, practical exercises, programmed instruction, questions and answers role-plays, simulations, and so on, selected appropriately to time, space and cost issues.

Technology can clearly make a valuable contribution, particularly in areas such as:

- technological advances;

- international business;

- environmental control.

A danger is to confuse instruction and training. Instruction contributes to training: it does not ensure learning. It may present or indeed challenge ideas, but it does not ensure a response.

Trainers consider how technology assistance can enhance learning. It may reduce costs, save time, and reinforce skills and knowledge – or it may not. It is a tool, not a panacea.

In fact, this assistance is central to continuing learning and development for individuals and organisations. It will be enhanced by increasingly effective technology. It will not be taken over or replaced on-line.

Why Bother?

Key questions are:

1.   Is e-learning cost effective?

      Compare design and development costs. A benefit balance is often seen when large numbers of participants are involved, particularly if they are widely dispersed geographically. Small numbers, easily assembled, may learn much better in face-to-face group meetings with a professional trainer.

2.   Can e-learning reduce time away from the job?

      Some information can clearly be given at the place of work, but there is a danger of constant interruption and distraction. Well-managed meetings still work and contribute to effective team building and motivational leadership.

3.   Can travel costs be reduced?

      The answer is clearly YES but perhaps at the cost of providing the stimulation of meeting people of varying backgrounds in different environments (if that is a reasonable and measurable objective in Mager's terms).

4.   Does 'web'-style information have more appeal and response in today's environment?

Books and classrooms are seen as old-fashioned sources of information by many younger people, but skilled trainers can move away from old-fashioned classroom ideas and with feeling, involvement and leadership.

Preparing for On-Line Training – Recognising the Constraints

On-line training is fashionable. Because of this, it is of special importance that cost-benefit questions are asked at a very early stage.

- What are the costs involved?

- Where are the savings?

- How do costs compare with other methods in the short and long term?

- Are there hidden costs?

- Where and when is it most appropriate?

- Is there a learning cost? For example, lack of questioning and interface with other learners?

- Are there unique benefits, for example, physical stimulation?

- Are there unique problems, for example, isolation?

Time – The Time Illusion

At national as well as organisational level, training is often seen as a cost rather than an investment in continuous improvement. This 'heads down' philosophy is, of course, a recipe for slow growth, slow learning and, often, decline. The training budget is seen as potential waste. On-line training investment is sometimes seen as part of this and sometimes as part of the counter-balancing solution. Workers can keep their heads down and learn on-line on the side. The answer is an integrated and well-balanced approach, recognising the need for balanced and integrated learning. On-line training is part of the answer, but rarely a complete recipe for meeting learning needs. Effectively combining learning and doing at all levels in an organisation is an ambition that may never be fully achieved, but it is still a legitimate goal.

Money

There is no recognised formula, as yet, for measuring the optimum investment in training, particularly on-line training. But data are emerging. The examples in the appendices are useful in terms of illustrating the scope and limits of application and impact.

The Business Case for Technology-Assisted Training

Technological advancement has made technology-assisted training possible. Speed of advance is very impressive – almost overwhelming. Trainers need to be knowledgeable to decide:

- Who needs it?

- What they need?

- When, where and how they receive it?

- At what cost?

There are also related ethical issues to be considered: is the latest expensive technology package being 'sold' because it is fashionable while it may or may not produce more effective learning?

With modern communication, trainers and trainees do not need to be together – in theory. The problem is that group training without a group 'present' can be stripped of nuance, emotion and intuitive learning, and be somewhat sterile.

The theory that call centres, for instance, should and could be based anywhere has some parallels. However, human communication and language are subtle. The results of flawed learning and communication can be irritating. Training and information exchange has to lead to improved competence. It is not just a question of factual exchange; communication is not just 'adult' understanding as defined by Eric Berne in his various works on Transactional Analysis. It involves feeling, particularly at the 'child' level. Learning to give information, without recognising the feelings surrounding the request, can lead to anger and frustration on both sides and result in the 'two-fingered response'. Knowledge management provides the basis for training and learning. Training is the process of using the knowledge base to achieve skilled performance. Some very advanced systems do translate knowledge into personal performance, as seen in the case of improving the effectiveness of wine sales personnel in California (see Appendix 16a).

E-Learning in Perspective

It is sometimes tempting to go for new approaches simply because they are good and modern. On this basis, a 'high-tech' approach can seem especially attractive simply because it appears to be avant-garde!

Unfortunately, in many cases it is very far from being cost effective. The key considerations are:

- What is the business need?

- What will work? And at what cost?

- How many people need training?

- How much time is available?

- What resources are available?

- Are trainers competent to use e-learning?

- What are the alternatives?

Many professional trainers know full well that e-learning can be surrounded by illusions. It is important to recognise these. Examples are:

- all training can be done on the Web;

- e-training always saves money;

- numbers trained can be unlimited;

- delivery on-line saves time;

- trainers and trainees can use the technology effectively;

- other methods are old fashioned and, therefore, ineffective;

- e-training is easier to evaluate.

The answers to these would have to be:

- it is easier to assess satisfaction;

- there is more understanding;

- more skills are developed, and so on.

So far, there can only be an 'non-proven' verdict. On-line training is an important part of the training mix. It cannot stand alone.

A practical approach for trainers deciding on priorities and possibilities is to carry out a 'Force Field Analysis' as illustrated in Appendix 16c.

Appendix 16a: Case Study

Many skills are clear and measureable. Unfortunately, many are not and it is in these areas that the value of e-training is most difficult to recognise and assess.

Examples are:

- sales skills;

- negotiation skills;

- multi-tasking;

- management skills, and so on.

An interesting development in the sales field comes from E.J. Gallo Winery in California.

The traditional approach has always been to teach sales skills in the setting the sales person will be using. Gallo's trainees were thousands of sales reps, widely scattered and often working from home. Bringing groups together for face-to-face training is inevitably time consuming and expensive.

The need was to save money without sacrificing the idea that training should focus on building practical skills rather than just delivering information. The need was not just 'content' but skill simulation – learning by doing.

After much searching, a design was produced, focussing on one red wine. The learner target group was straight from college with little or no knowledge of wine. The training objective was to bring the trainees quickly to a point where they could:

- walk confidently into a fine wine shop;

- interact with the owner;

- make a well-targeted, well-planned sales presentation;

- discuss positioning of the product in the store;

- outline promotional opportunities;

- follow up on the sale to ensure that 'everything is done properly so that the wine is profitable to the retailer' (Rothwell, 2006).

The programme had to cover the basics of wine production, tasting, the mechanics of sniffing and swirling and why these are important. This part of the course was informational, not simulated; practising actual tasting can certainly not be done via the Internet. Audio segments, however, included a professional pitch to a retailer, with the learner following the text on a screen. Skill-building modules walked the learner through the sales process. The producers referred to this as 'simulation'.

This may be arguable, but it certainly gave the learners a chance to practise skills in a context similar to the real world and provide interactive elements in the learning.

Following the pilot training, distribution points increased 30 per cent compared with controlled experience. A four-month increase in actual sales was 25 per cent higher in the training markets.

This was seen as successful training. It was certainly e-learning. Apparently it paid off.

Appendix 16b: On-Line Training in a Large, Multi-National Organisation

THE THALES EXPERIENCE

The Thales Group have a wealth of experience in managing multi-million pound projects on a global scale. Generalist and specialist training is offered on an international basis. They lead the field in terms of on-line learning and training. Help and information is available from their bases in Crawley and Basingstoke in the UK and six other centres worldwide – Hengelo, Jouy-en-Joses, Rome, Stuttgart, Sydney and Washington DC.

Information in this Appendix has been obtained from the Thales University in Crawley. The use of e-learning has developed steadily since 1990, e-training is seen as part of this investment in learning and the development of people.

Investment in training is seen as about 3 per cent of payroll with about 0.5 per cent spent on e-learning. The company has a very strong HR culture of which training is a major part.

This training has been carefully costed with investment in major e-learning projects running at around £20,000 each. Training involving e-learning is seen as 'blended learning'. In many cases, high-tech training develops alongside more traditional approaches; 35 per cent of e-learning is seen as 'high tech' with a blend moving towards a preponderance of more traditional training at senior management levels, emphasising leadership, influencing skills, and so on.

The company has no doubt that e-training at the appropriate level has financial advantages in a widely dispersed organisation where travel costs are high and that time in their 'universities', while essential, has to be limited.

The Thales experience begs the question of 'What is the distinction between e-learning and e-training?'. On balance, the picture is one of a broad personal development approach within which is a clear recognition of the need, in hard-nosed financial terms, for certain essential and developing skills to be promoted and available to the organisation. This is training – for profit. It has been costed and evaluated and also makes a broader contribution to the culture and philosophy of the organisation. Evaluation has been in financial, developmental and human terms.

Contact:
Thales University
Sackville House
Gatwick Road
Crawley
West Sussex
RH10 9RL, UK
http://intranet.uk.corp.thales/university_uk

Appendix 16c: Force-Field Analysis Exercise as might be Applied to use of On-Line Training in an Organisation

OBJECTIVE: the promotion of effective and profitable on-line training.

Each force should now be considered in terms of increasing the power of the driving forces and reducing the power of the restraining forces (often in discussion with a group) and might result in the following 'action needed' list:

- publicity (as in Thales, see Appendix 16b);

- enhance computer competence;

- establish easy access;

- promote related short group sessions;

- involve top management and line managers;

- agree realistic budgets;

- recruit high-potential staff (for example, Gallo Winery);

- enhance existing training skills;

- select high quality, fair price hardware/software providers;

- train trainers;

- broadcast results;

- monitor competitors;

- promote the training profession, for example, Thales 'Universities' (see Appendix 16b).

DRIVING FORCES	RESTRAINING FORCES
modern ideas	impersonal
time saving	limited feedback
cost reduction: travel and so on	lack of team building
customer acceptance	development costs
line management support	limited management understanding
professional training	lack of incentive
	poor selection of participants
	and so on

The Last Word?

Most often, in paradigms of the training or learning process, the last word or activity, is 'EVALUATION'.

For example, the main tenets of the Investors in People Standard are listed as:

- Commitment

- Planning

- Action

- Evaluation

Moreover, many training courses end their session with some sort of questionnaire, which at best, elicits comment on the perceived 'quality' of the presentations, and at worst, is a 'clapometer' describing how much we liked the trainer, the facilities and the food, or how impressed or unimpressed we were with the 'Death by Powerpoint' approach.

So, how do we evaluate a learning experience to assess whether it was worth the cost?

First, we must decide on what outcome we want on the part of an individual or group. What do we want them to do more or better, or perhaps stop doing? Note the use of the verb 'to do,' for it is impossible to measure (evaluate) accurately anything which is not observable. Beware, whether designing a learning experience, or selecting a training course from a provider, woolly and imprecise terms, such as:

- to have a grasp of…

- to understand the importance of...

- to develop an appreciation of...

- to know how...

- to improve attitudes...

The above are at least 'learner centred' and could be amplified by stating conditions under which desired performance would give evidence, for example, of 'understanding'.

Again, beware!

An objective might be described as: 'to demonstrate understanding of the ISO 9001 standard by listing the various clauses'. BUT, how much more valuable is the stated objective of: 'be able to conduct Internal Audits of the ISO 9000 System and write written reports to the satisfaction of the Registration Body'?...and even better, to add: 'and which make a significant contribution to continual improvement in the organisation'.

There is a plethora of opportunities to measure the success of that objective and it is hard work, but the final outcome is worth the effort and ultimately costs less.

In Robert Mager's *Preparing Instructional Objectives*, these principles are outlined eloquently and with much wit and wisdom. This is a programmed learning text, which also demonstrates the maxim of 'don't teach them anything they know (how to do!) already'.

When thinking about improved performance or the 'performance gap,' we must ask whether the person 'used to be able' to do the task. If the answer is 'yes,' then we must consider what has happened, is practice necessary or do we have obstacles in a motivational sense?

Ken Blanchard addresses this issue in his 'Situational Leadership' model. The individual who falls into the category of 'High Competence/Variable Performance' needs to be helped with the 'Supportive' leadership approach of asking questions to identify problems which are preventing acceptable performance.

A live example of this was exhibited in an organisation which, for operational reasons, had crews out and about, placing traffic cones to identify the presence of road works. They had been trained, or simply instructed, as to what height of cones were appropriate in which situations, for example, motorways, dual carriageways, country lanes, and so on. The local police were constantly complaining that the wrong sizes were being used.

The company response was to organise a 'training programme' (a 'refresher' maybe?) and naturally improvement was short lived. Instead of incurring more costs, training venue, time off, wages of those attending, and so on, an enlightened Manager, straight from the Blanchard seminar, started to ask some questions. It transpired there was a planning problem, in that those who loaded the vans with cones were not fully aware of the requirements of the roads. In addition, having discovered the problem, frequently close to the end of the day, the drivers were impeded from returning to base, some 20 or 30 miles away by a ban on overtime. Not a training problem, except, perhaps, for senior management! So we might start again with 'what performance needs to be changed?'

Finally, training may not be a last resort, but if selected as a solution to improved performance, must be rigorously subjected to an examination of whether it is designed in response to, and can achieve the stated objectives, which must be observable and measurable, and that the means for this evaluation have been designed as the first step and not the last.

An erstwhile European Commissioner was heard to have said: 'If you don't know where you're going, for sure you're going to get there!' and Robert Mager echoes this in his Sea Horse fable.

Various methods of analysis and techniques are discussed in detail elsewhere in this book, and all can be enhanced by attention to knowing where we are going before employing them.

Bibliography

Books recommended for basic reading are marked with an asterisk.

Allen, K.R., 'Value for money in training,' *Technical Education*, 5 (1963).

Bacie, 'A standard method of costing the training of apprentices,' *Bacie Journal*, 17 (1963) 102–4.

Barany, J.W., 'A prediction model for reduction of retraining costs,' *Work Study*, 17 (5 May 1968) 7–13, 25.

Bass, B.M. and Vaughan, J.A., *Training in Industry – The Management of Learning* (London, Tavistock Publications; Belmont, CA, Wadsworth Publishing Co Inc, 1967).

Berne, E., *Games People Play* (New York: Grove Press, 1964).

Bernstein, P.L., *Against the Gods* (New York: John Wiley, 1996).

Borus, M.E., 'A benefit-cost analysis of the economic effectiveness of retraining the unemployed,' *Yale Economic Essays*, 4 (1964) 370.

Bossman, O., 'The cost of further training: an important element in its provision,' *Arbeit und Arbeitsrecht*, 22 (1967) 351–9.

Brockman, J.R., *Trained and Untrained Substitutability, Productivity and Costs* (Bromley, Kent, Ministry of Defence Library 1989).

Catalanello, R.F. and Kirkpatrick, D.L., 'Evaluating training programs: the state of the art,' *Training and Development Journal*, 22 (5 May 1968) 2–9.

CIRF, Training for progress: evaluating supervisory training, number 4 (ILO, 1965).

*City and Guilds of London Institute, *Further Education for Craftsmen* (1964).

*City and Guilds of London Institute, *Further Education for Operatives* (1964).

*City and Guilds of London Institute, *Further Education for Technicians* (1964).

Dale, A.J., 'Whatever happened to common skills?' *Industrial Training International*, 3 (1968).

Davidson, A.F., 'Budgeting for industrial training,' *Management Accounting* (1967) 6–11.

Diaz-Vazquez, P., 'On-the-job training, firing costs and employment,' Discussion paper (London, Centre for Economic Policy Research, 2004).

Dixon, M., 'How to prove that training can pay,' *The Guardian* (19 December 1967).

Dockery, M., 'The cost of apprenticeship training in Australia' (CLMR, Curtin University of Technology, 1996).

Doyle, L.F., 'An evaluation of apprenticeship: growth or stagnation,' *Training and Development Journal*, 21 (10 October 1967), 2–12.

Drouet, P., 'Vocational training costs: result of a pilot study and an essay in methodology,' *International Labour Review*, 97 (Geneva, 1968).

Edwards, J.E., Scott, J.C. and Raju, N.S., *The Human Resources Program-Evaluation Handbook* (Thousand Oaks, CA; London, Sage Publications c2003).

Elkin, G., 'Exploring the environment, discovering learning resources and creating low cost training' (Cranfield School of Management, 1990).

Ellis, C.D. and Talbot, J.R., *Analysis and Costing of Company Training* (Aldershot, Gower Press, 1969).

Forrester, D.A.R., 'Costs and benefits of industrial training,' *Technical Education* 2 (1967) 60–5.

Garbutt, D., 'Determination of training costs,' *Accountant* (February 1967) 11–18.

Gauchet, F., *et al.*, 'Evaluation of effects of supervisory training,' *Interproductivite*, Supplement to number 144 (1967).

Georgiades, N., *et al.*, 'Management training; evaluation within the organisation,' *Bulletin of the British Psychological Society*, 21 (1968) 104.

Hamblin, A.C., *The Evaluation and Control of Training* (London, McGraw-Hill, 1974). (One of the few published books specifically devoted to evaluation, it is intended to be a link between how-to-do-it approaches and theoretical dissertations. Hamblin aims the book at training specialists and bases his discussions on a cycle of evaluation of objectives and effects. A range of techniques at each level is discussed.)

Helbing, J.D., 'Critical requirements in evaluating,' *Flight Safety*, 1(2) (1967) 10–16.

Henry, J., 'Cost factors affecting the future of IT-based training' (Open University, Teaching and Consultancy Centre, 1991).

Henshaw, P., 'The costs and benefits of training – an annotated bibliography' (University of Warwick for MSC, 1987).

Herbert, N., 'Assessing training costs,' *Industrial Training International*, 2 (1967) 516–22.

Herzberg, F., *Work and the Nature of Man* (London, Staples Press, 1968).

Hesseling, P., 'Strategy of evaluation research in the field of supervisory and management training' (Assen, Van Gorcum and Company, 1996).

Hillman, H.A., 'Measuring management training: a case study,' *Journal of the American Society of Training Directors*, 16(3) (March 1962) 27–31.

Hogarth, T., 'The net costs of training to employers' (Department for Education and Employment HMSO, 1996).

Hogarth, T., 'Employers' net costs of training to NVQ level 2' (Department of Education and Employment RR, 1998)

Hogarth, T., 'Net costs of modern apprenticeship training to employers' (Nottingham, Department of Education and Skills, 2003).

Holding, D.H., *Principles of Training* (Oxford, Pergamon Press, 1965).

Horowitz, M.A., *et al.*, 'Evaluation of training in Brazil,' *CIKF Training for Progress*, 5 (1966).

Humble, J., *Improving Management Performance* (London, British Institute of Management, 1965).

Institute Of Personnel Management, Costing the training function: report of a conference (1965).

Jahoda, M. and Barnitz, E., 'The nature of evaluation,' *International Social Science Journal*, 7 (1955) 353–64.

Jones, I.S., 'A study of the net cost to employers of providing work experience and training' (National Economic Research Associates, 1987, 1992).

Keating, E.G., *Cost Comparisons on DoD Education and Training* (Santa Monica, CA, Rand, 2006).

Kepner, C.H. and Tregoe, B.B., *The Rational Manager* (New York, McGraw-Hill 1965).

King, D., *Training within the Organisation* (London, Tavistock Publications, 1964).

King, S.D.M., 'Automation and the evaluation of training,' *International Labour Review*, xc (1964) 209–25.

Kirkpatrick, D., 'Techniques for evaluating training programs,' *Journal of the American Society of Training Directors*, 13(11) (November 1959), 3–9; 13(12) (December 1959), 21–6; 14(1) (January 1960), 13–8; 14(2) (February 1960), 28–32.

Kirkpatrick, D., 'How to evaluate training programs,' *Journal of the American Society of Training Directors*, 14 (1960) 21–3.

Kropp, R.P. and Hankin, E.K., 'Paper and pencil tests for evaluating instruction,' *Journal of the American Society of Training Directors*, 16(11) (November 1962) 25–35.

Lerda, L.W. and Cross, L.W., 'Performance-orientated training,' *Training Directors Journal*, 15(11) (November 1961); 17(4) (April 1963).

Local Government Examinations Board, *Memorandum on the Costs of Training* (1966).

London, M., *Managing the Training Enterprise, Cost-Effective Training in Organisations* (San Francisco, CA: Jossey-Bass Publishers, 1989).

Mager, R.F., *Preparing Instructional Objectives* (Atlanta, GA, Center for Effective Performance Inc, 3rd edition, 1997).

Mahoney, T.A., 'Evaluation of training.' *Personnel*, 30 (1960) 334–45.

Markwell, D.S. and Roberts, T.J., *Organisation of Management Development Programmes* (London, Gower Press, 1969).

Maynard, H.B., Stegemerten, G.J. and Schwab, J.L., *Methods-Time Measurement* (New York, McGraw-Hill, 1948).

Mcclelland, D.C., *The Achieving Society* (Princeton, D van Nostrand, 1961).

McKnight, A.J. and Hunter, H.G., 'An experimental evaluation of a driver simulator for safety training,' *HUMBRO Professional Paper*, number 9–66 (1966).

McMahon, F.A., *The Great Training Robbery* (New York, Falmer, 1990).

Meaklim, T.P., *The Cost and Benefits of Training with the Police Service in Northern Ireland* (University of Hull, 2002).

Moore, W.R., 'Training evaluation – it used to be simple,' *New York Training Directors Journal*, 18(4) (April 1964) 45–50.

Murdick, R.G., 'Measuring the profit in industry training programs,' *Journal of the American Society of Training Directors,* 14(4) (April 1960) 23–9.

Nelson, J., 'Criteria for choice project,' *Industrial Training International* (November 1966) 353–7; (March 1967) 124–8.

Newby, T., *Cost-Effective Training* (London, Kogan Page, 1992).

Odiorne, G.S., 'Evaluation of management training – what do we know about it,' *Journal of the American Society of Training Directors*, 13(1) (October 1959) 32–6.

Phillips, J.J., *Costs and ROI – Evaluation at the Ultimate Level* (Pfeiffer, San Franscisco, CA, John Wiley (distributor) 2008).

Phillips, J.S., *The Value of Learning: How Organisations Capture Value and ROI and Translate it into Support, Improvement, and Funds* (Jossey-Bass, Chichester, John Wiley (distributor) 2007).

Phillips, P., Strategies for implementation of HR and training – cost effectiveness (Burlington, MA. Buttersworth-Heineman, 2007).

Phillips, P.P., *Understanding the Basics of Return on Investment in Training* (London, Kogan Page, 2002).

Pond, B., Performance on file, how to supervise. Test before and after supervisory training (unpublished, Pennsylvania State College, 1961).

Rae, L., *How to Measure Training Effectiveness* (Aldershot, Gower Publishing Company Limited, 1997).

Revans, R.N., *The Origins and Growth of Action Learning* (Bromley, Chartwell-Bratt Ltd, 1982).

Robinson, J. and Barnes, N. (eds), *New Media and Methods in Industrial Training* (London, BBC, 1967).

Rolfe, J.M., 'Evaluation of visual displays, techniques and trends,' *Occupational Psychology*, 41 (1967) 49.

Rose, H.C., 'A plan for training evaluation,' *Training and Development Journal*, 22(5) (May 1968) 38–51.

Rothwell, J.R., *The Handbook of Training Technologies* (San Francisco, CA, Pfeiffer, 2006).

Rufsuold, M.I., 'Guides to the selection and evaluation of newer educational media,' *Audiovisual Instruction*, 12 (1967) 10–15.

Sewell, D.O., 'A critique of cost/benefit analysis of training,' *Monthly Labor Review* (September 1967) 45–51.

Seymour, W.D., *Industrial Skills* (London, Pitman, 1966).

Seymour, W.D., *Skills Analysis Training* (London, Pitman, 1968).

Shaffer, D.E., 'Control through measurement,' *Training Directors Journal*, 18(9) (September 1964) 39–50.

Shirley-Smith, K., *Programmed Learning in Integrated Industrial Training* (London, Gower Press, 1968).

Spencer, L.M., *Calculating Human Resource Costs and Benefits* (New York, Wiley 1986).

Stepanov, B. and Birg, V., 'An economic evaluation of vocational training,' *Professional 'no techniceskoe Obrayovanie,'* 24(12) (December 1967) 29.

Toynbee, A.J., *A Study of History* (Oxford, Oxford University Press, 1947).

Thurley, K.E., 'Evaluating supervisory and management training,' *ATM Bulletin*, 7(5) (December 1967) 43–55.

Training and Development Journal, 'Evaluating to reduce training costs' (January 1967).

Tucker, B. (ed.), 'Cost effectiveness of open and flexible learning' (Department of Education and Employment, 1996).

Warr, P. *et al.*, 'Evaluating management training,' *ATM Bulletin*, 8(2) (July 1968) 1–13.

Warr, P.B, Bird, M. and Rackham, N., *The Evaluation of Management Training* (London, Gower, 1970). (One of the few books devoted to the subject. It offers a strongly practical approach to validation and evaluation, identifying the needs in a framework called CIRO which emphasises context, input, reaction and outcome evaluation, the latter having three levels of immediate, intermediate and ultimate outcomes.)

Weisbrod, B.A., 'Conceptual issues in evaluating training programs,' *Monthly Labor Review,* 89(10) (October 1996) 1091–7.

Willis, J.E. and Dow, A.N., *Quantification of Personnel Performance for Cost Effectiveness Decisions; An Annotated Bibliography,* San Diego, Naval Personnel Research Activity, Contract RM SRM 67–15 (1967).

Index

If you have found this book useful you may be interested in other titles from Gower

Global HR:
Challenges Facing the Function
Peter Reilly and Tony Williams
Hardback: 978-1-4094-0278-7
ebook: 978-1-4094-0279-4

Talent Assessment:
A New Strategy for Talent Management
Tony Davis with Maggie Cutt, Neil Flynn, Peter Mowl and Simon Orme
Hardback: 978-0-566-08731-8
ebook: 978-0-7546-8895-2

Six Sigma in HR Transformation:
Achieving Excellence in Service Delivery
Mircea Albeanu and Ian Hunter with Jo Radford
Hardback: 978-0-566-09164-3
ebook: 978-0-566-09165-0

Cultural Differences and Improving Performance:
How Values and Beliefs Influence Organizational
Performance
Bryan Hopkins
Hardback: 978-0-566-08907-7
ebook: 978-0-566-08908-4

GOWER

Informal Learning:
A New Model for Making Sense of Experience
Lloyd Davies
Hardback: 978-0-566-08857-5

Electronic Performance Support:
Using Digital Technology to Enhance Human Ability
Edited by
Philip Barker and Paul van Schaik
Hardback: 978-0-566-08884-1
ebook: 978-0-566-09239-8

Visit **www.gowerpublishing.com** and

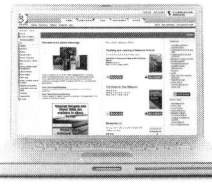

- search the entire catalogue of Gower books in print
- order titles online at 10% discount
- take advantage of special offers
- sign up for our monthly e-mail update service
- download free sample chapters from all recent titles
- download or order our catalogue